I0214233

# Ancestors and Descendants of Peter Paul Cabay and Dorothy Lucille Quinn of Detroit

# Ancestors and Descendants of Peter Paul Cabay and Dorothy Lucille Quinn of Detroit

Christopher D. Cook

Silver Anchor Press : 2025

Published in 2025 by Silver Anchor Press, Berrien Springs, Michigan

ISBN 978-0-9991137-3-8

This work is licensed under Creative Commons Attribution-
NonCommercial-ShareAlike 4.0 International
https://creativecommons.org/licenses/by-nc-sa/4.0
(Some images may have different licenses: see Illustration Credits)

Available online at: https://archive.org/details/9780999113738

*For Jackson, Mason, Liv, Aidan, Lily,*
*and those yet to come.*

# Contents

# Introduction

Peter Paul Cabay and Dorothy Lucille Quinn were both born in Detroit in 1927, the children of immigrants. While their parents came from different countries—Peter's from Poland and Dorothy's from Ireland—their ancestors for generations shared remarkably similar experiences of conquest, famine, disease, poverty, peasant life, and faith in the Catholic Church. And yet, despite extraordinary hardship, these ancestors' offspring survived to venture across the Atlantic Ocean with the courage to leave behind all that was familiar, full of hope for a better life, albeit a hard-earned one, in the United States. In 1950, Peter and Dorothy married, uniting their Polish and Irish heritage into a "melting pot" story shared by millions of American families. Today, their descendants continue their story into the twenty-first century.

## About this Book

This book records Peter Paul Cabay's and Dorothy Lucille Quinn's lineal ancestors and those ancestors' children; earlier and later marriages and half-siblings are generally not included but are mentioned in some cases. Most of the Polish ancestry was compiled from indexes (primarily Geneteka and *Poland, Church Books, 1568–1990*) as the relevant primary documents are not widely available. Irish genealogy is notoriously difficult owing to naming conventions and record loss, therefore Irish families in this book may not include all children. To respect the privacy of living people their places of birth and dates of birth have been omitted; only birth years are given.

## Names

Polish is an inflected language meaning the form of a word—including names—changes depending on a variety of factors including the word's grammatical function, whether it is singular or plural, or whether it is masculine, feminine, or neuter. Some surnames of women could also have suffixes indicating whether they are married or unmarried. Using the surname Szymaszek as an example, Szymaszkówna means "unmarried daughter of Szymaszek" while Szymaszkowa means "wife or widow of Szymaszek." For the sake of simplicity, the masculine singular form of Polish surnames is used in this book with acknowledgment that this is grammatically incorrect in the Polish language.[1]

Most parish records of the Catholic Church were written in Latin until well into the twentieth century. In this book names have been given in English or Polish rather than the Latin in which they appear in records.

## Places

To save space several frequently used placenames are not given in the usual full genealogical style of *place, district, region, country* but rather are shortened to just place:

*Ardoughan*, a townland in County Mayo, Ireland
*Ballina*, a town in County Mayo, Ireland
*Cloghan*, a town in County Offaly, Ireland
*Detroit*, a city in Wayne County, Michigan, United States
*Glinik*, a village in Ropczyce-Sędziszów County, Podkarpackie Province, Poland
*Łączki Kucharskie*, a parish in Ropczyce-Sędziszów County, Podkarpackie Province, Poland
*Lubzina*, a parish in Ropczyce-Sędziszów County, Podkarpackie Province, Poland
*Lumcloon*, a townland in County Offaly, Ireland
*Paszczyna*, a village in Dębica County, Podkarpackie Province, Poland
*Wola Brzeźnicka*, a village in Dębica County, Podkarpackie Province, Poland

## Families

To aid in organization and navigation, families are numbered by surname and chronologically. For example, the first Cabaj family in this book is numbered C-1. Family numbers are also color coded: Polish are red, Irish green, and American blue.

# Family Tree Charts

The family tree charts on the following pages organize visually the families described in this book. The charts may be read chronologically left to right with each subsequent generation occupying its own column. Ancestors and siblings of Peter Paul Cabay are presented first, then ancestors and siblings of Dorothy Lucille Quinn, and finally their descendants.

# Ancestors of Peter Paul Cabay

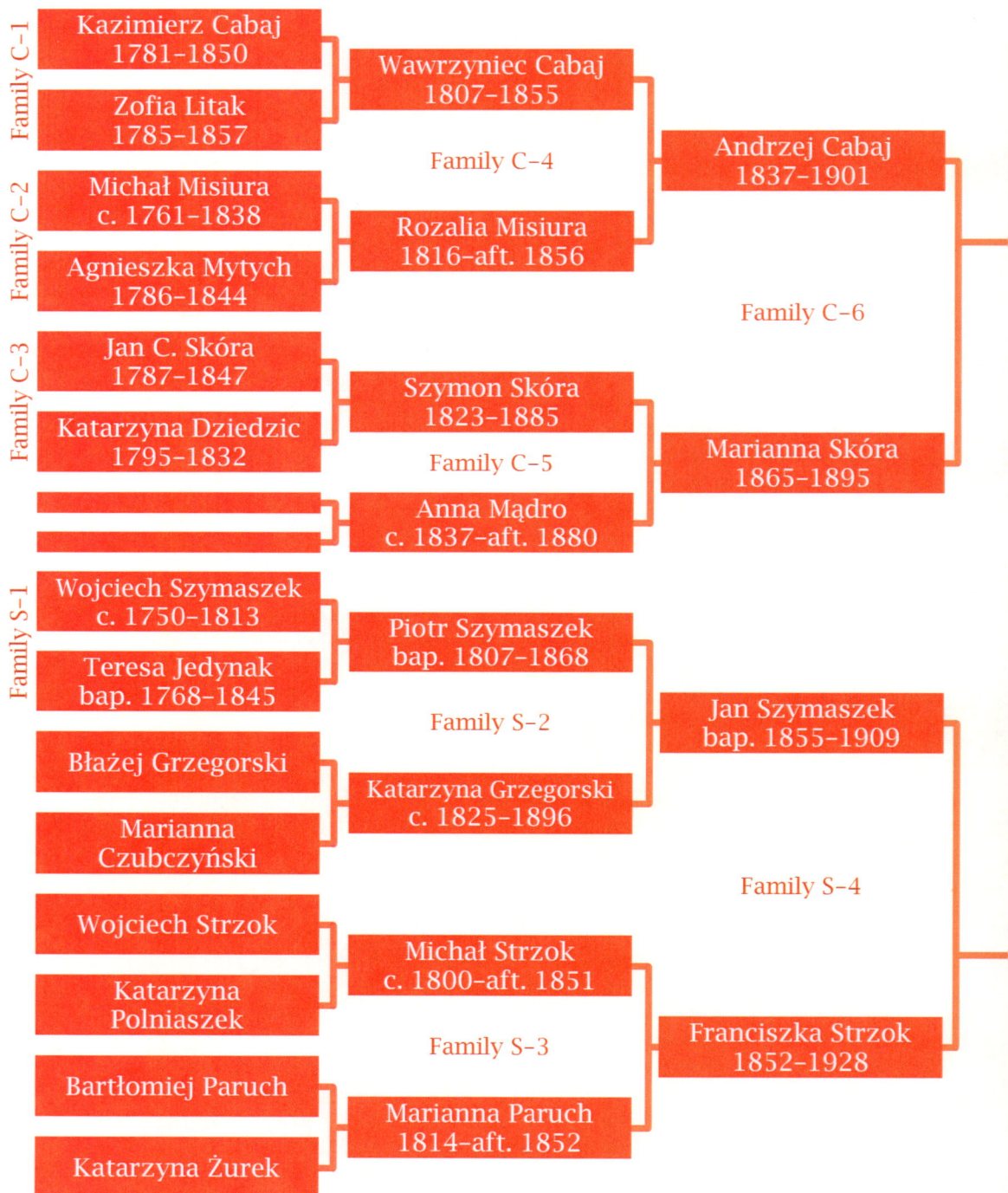

**Family C-1**

Kazimierz Cabaj
1781–1850

Zofia Litak
1785–1857

Wawrzyniec Cabaj
1807–1855

Family C-4

**Family C-2**

Michał Misiura
c. 1761–1838

Agnieszka Mytych
1786–1844

Rozalia Misiura
1816–aft. 1856

Andrzej Cabaj
1837–1901

Family C-6

**Family C-3**

Jan C. Skóra
1787–1847

Katarzyna Dziedzic
1795–1832

Szymon Skóra
1823–1885

Family C-5

Anna Mądro
c. 1837–aft. 1880

Marianna Skóra
1865–1895

**Family S-1**

Wojciech Szymaszek
c. 1750–1813

Teresa Jedynak
bap. 1768–1845

Piotr Szymaszek
bap. 1807–1868

Family S-2

Błażej Grzegorski

Marianna
Czubczyński

Katarzyna Grzegorski
c. 1825–1896

Jan Szymaszek
bap. 1855–1909

Family S-4

Wojciech Strzok

Katarzyna
Polniaszek

Michał Strzok
c. 1800–aft. 1851

Family S-3

Bartłomiej Paruch

Katarzyna Żurek

Marianna Paruch
1814–aft. 1852

Franciszka Strzok
1852–1928

# Parents and Siblings of Peter Paul Cabay

Władysław "Walter" Cabaj
1889–1976

Joseph Anthony Cabaj
1915–2003

Alphonse Cabaj
1917–1918

Clara Theresa Cabay
1919–1994

Cecelia Helen Cabay
1922–2016

Mary Magdalene Cabay
1925–1992

Peter Paul Cabay
1927–1999

Bernard Cabaj
1929–1929

Eugene John Cabaj
1930–2009

Family C–7

Leokadia "Eleanore" Szymaszek
1893–1974

An ➡ signifies that person had one or more children

# Ancestors of Dorothy Lucille Quinn

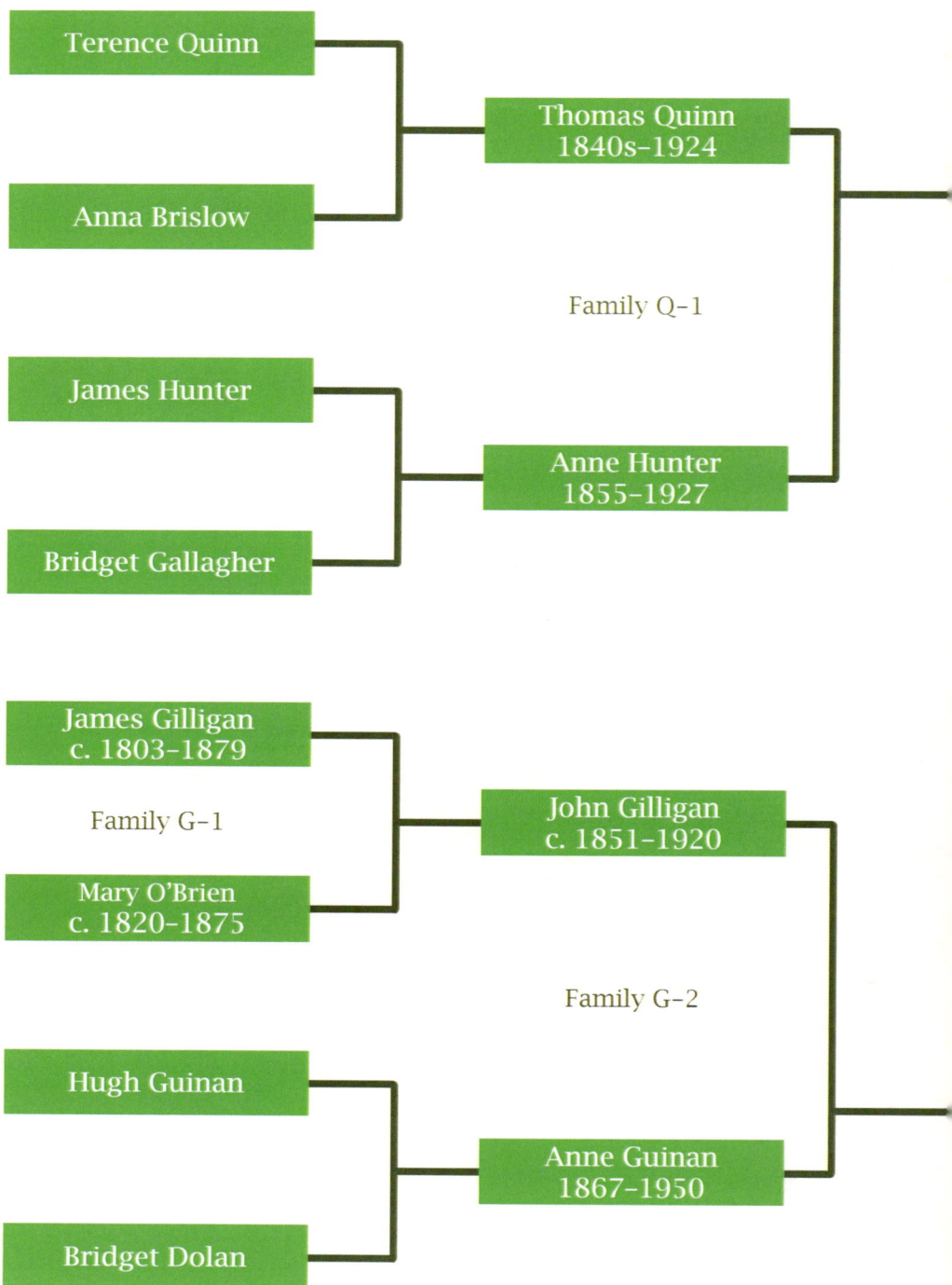

Terence Quinn

Anna Brislow

Thomas Quinn
1840s–1924

Family Q–1

James Hunter

Bridget Gallagher

Anne Hunter
1855–1927

James Gilligan
c. 1803–1879

Family G–1

Mary O'Brien
c. 1820–1875

John Gilligan
c. 1851–1920

Family G–2

Hugh Guinan

Bridget Dolan

Anne Guinan
1867–1950

# Parents and Siblings of Dorothy Lucille Quinn

**John Joseph Quinn**
**1882–1962**

Family Q–2

**Anne Marie Quinn**
**1913–1994** →

**Margaret Cecelia Quinn**
**1914–2001** →

**Thomas James Quinn**
**1916–1993** →

**Helen Agnes Quinn**
**1918–1997** →

**John Joseph Quinn, Jr.**
**1919–1996** →

**Catherine E. Quinn**
**1921–1979** →

**William Quinn**
**1923–1923**

**Joseph Michael Quinn**
**1924–1986** →

**Agnes Elizabeth Quinn**
**1925–2000** →

**Dorothy Lucille Quinn**
**1927–2010** →

**James Francis Quinn**
**1928–1992**

**Mary Gilligan**
**1890–1991**

An → signifies that person had one or more children

# Descendants of Peter Paul Cabay and Dorothy Lucille Quinn

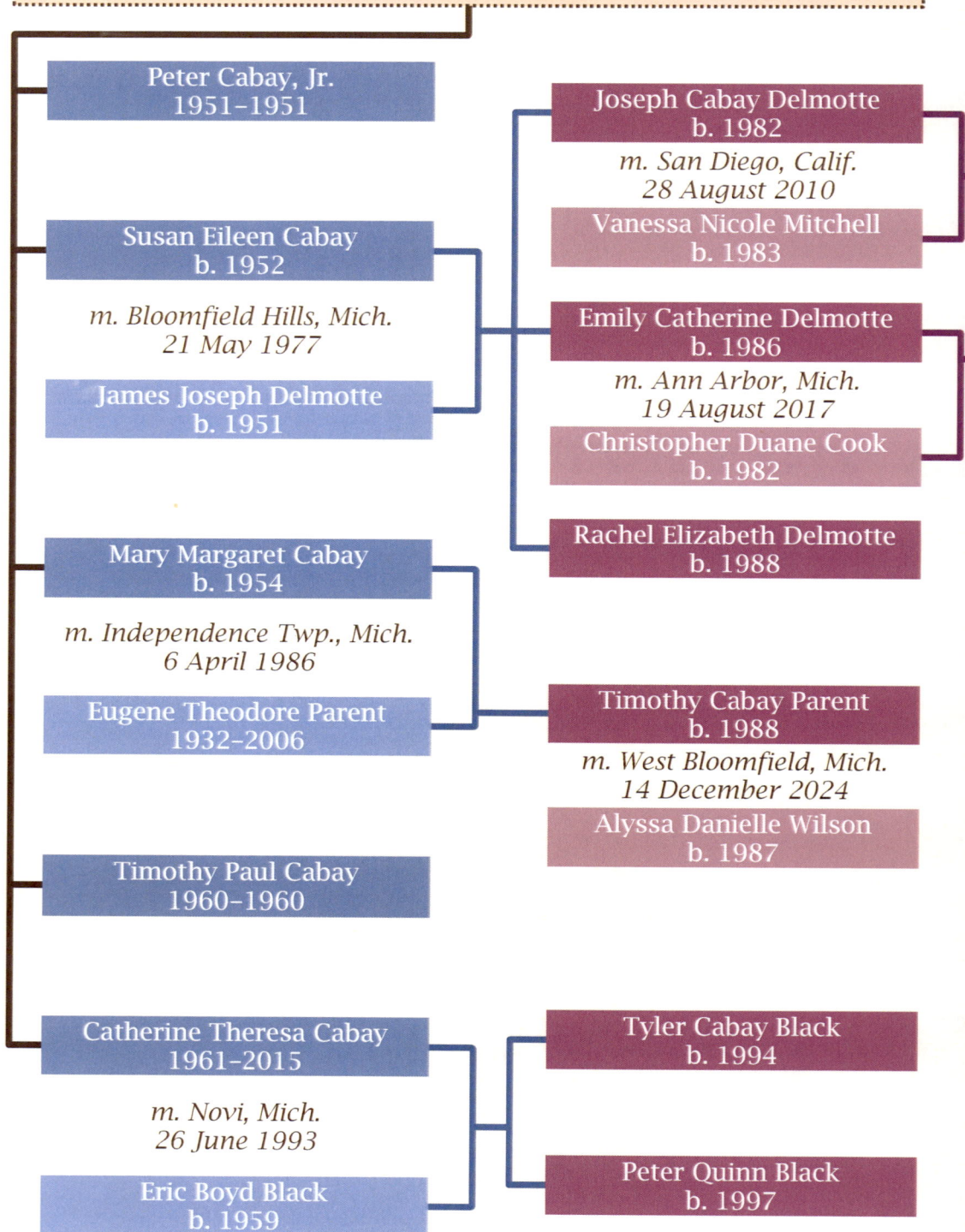

**Peter Cabay, Jr.**
1951–1951

**Susan Eileen Cabay**
b. 1952

*m. Bloomfield Hills, Mich.*
*21 May 1977*

**James Joseph Delmotte**
b. 1951

**Joseph Cabay Delmotte**
b. 1982

*m. San Diego, Calif.*
*28 August 2010*

**Vanessa Nicole Mitchell**
b. 1983

**Emily Catherine Delmotte**
b. 1986

*m. Ann Arbor, Mich.*
*19 August 2017*

**Christopher Duane Cook**
b. 1982

**Rachel Elizabeth Delmotte**
b. 1988

**Mary Margaret Cabay**
b. 1954

*m. Independence Twp., Mich.*
*6 April 1986*

**Eugene Theodore Parent**
1932–2006

**Timothy Cabay Parent**
b. 1988

*m. West Bloomfield, Mich.*
*14 December 2024*

**Alyssa Danielle Wilson**
b. 1987

**Timothy Paul Cabay**
1960–1960

**Catherine Theresa Cabay**
1961–2015

*m. Novi, Mich.*
*26 June 1993*

**Eric Boyd Black**
b. 1959

**Tyler Cabay Black**
b. 1994

**Peter Quinn Black**
b. 1997

Jackson Patrick Delmotte
b. 2014

Mason James Delmotte
b. 2014

Liv Sue Delmotte
b. 2018

Aidan James Cook
b. 2020

Lily Susannah Cook
b. 2024

*The Spirit of Detroit.*

Location within Poland

Wola Brzeźnicka
Paszczyna
Lubzina
Łączki Kucharskie
Glinik

Podkarpackie Province, Poland

Ukraine

Slovakia

0                    Miles                    50

# Background: Poland

Peter Paul Cabay was the son of Władysław "Walter" Cabaj and Leokadia "Eleanore" Szymaszek, both immigrants from southeastern Poland. When Walter and Eleanore were born in the late 1800s, their part of Poland—known then as Galicia—had been under the control of Austria for a century. Other parts of what is modern Poland were controlled by the Prussian and Russian empires and attempts at independence were unsuccessful. Poverty, famine, low employment, and overpopulation were widespread problems which resulted in mass emigration.

By 1920, millions of people had emigrated from Austrian, Prussian, and Russian Polish lands to the United States seeking opportunities for better lives. Large populations settled in New York City, Buffalo, Pittsburgh, Cleveland, Detroit, Chicago, and the coal mining regions of Pennsylvania. In these new places, the immigrants lived together in tight-knit communities where they maintained their language, religion, and traditions. This Polish diaspora in the United States came to be called Polonia.[2]

A Polish village about 1880 (Ludwik Kurella, *W małym miasteczku*).

# The Cabaj Family in Poland

Peter Cabay's paternal ancestors came from the village of Glinik in the parish of Łączki Kucharskie in what is now Ropczyce-Sędziszów County, Podkarpackie Province, Poland. Glinik is situated on the Wielopolka River in the northern foothills of the Carpathian Mountains about 70 miles east of Kraków. The area is made up of rolling farm fields and scattered forests.

The Cabaj surname appears in records of Podkarpackie Province at least as early as 1715, sometimes spelled as Czabaj, Czabay, Czaboj, and variations thereof.[3] The surname is of uncertain origin, perhaps from a Ukrainian word or borrowed, via Ukrainian, from Turkish *czoban* meaning "Turkish or Wallachian shepherd." Outside of Poland it is also found as Cabai or Cabay.[4]

### FAMILY C-1

**Kazimierz Cabaj** was born to Grzegorz Cabaj and Agnieszka (Cudecka) Cabaj on 27 February 1781 in Glinik and died there on 9 March 1850.[5] He married **Zofia Litak** on 10 February 1806 in Glinik.[6] She was born to Szymon Litak and Zofia (Szarek) Litak on 12 April 1785 in Glinik and died there on 13 April 1857.[7]

Known children of Kazimierz Cabaj and Zofia (Litak) Cabaj, all born in Glinik:[8]

Wawrzyniec Cabaj, b. 3 August 1807, d. 20 July 1855 [Family C-4]
Katarzyna Cabaj, b. 10 November 1811
Marianna Cabaj, b. 23 March 1815
Zofia Cabaj, b. 1 May 1817
Józef Cabaj, b. 5 March 1819
Franciszka Cabaj, b. 11 February 1821, d. 9 February 1871

Anna Cabaj, b. 18 March 1824
Józef Cabaj, b. and d. 1 January 1828
Franciszek Cabaj, b. 27 March 1829, d. 7 January 1892

## FAMILY C-2

**Michał Misiura** was born to Adam Misiura and Jadwiga (Wiktor) Misiura about 1761 or 1762 probably in or near Glinik and died there on 15 November 1838.[9] He married **Agnieszka Mytych** on 23 November 1801 in Glinik.[10] She was born to Krzysztof Mytych and Jadwiga (Mazur) Mytych on 5 February 1786 probably in or near Glinik and died there on 4 April 1844.[11]

Known children of Michał Misiura and Agnieszka (Mytych) Misiura, all born in Glinik:[12]

Szymon Misiura, b. 13 October 1802
Katarzyna Misiura, b. 18 October 1803
Marianna Misiura, b. 1 December 1805
Agnieszka Misiura, b. 9 January 1809
Wojciech Misiura, b. 10 April 1811
Wiktoria Misiura, b. 19 December 1812
Jan Misiura, b. 23 June 1815 (twin)
Paweł Misiura, b. 23 June 1815 (twin)
Rozalia "Róża" Misiura, b. 6 August 1816, d. after 13 February 1856 [Family C-4]
Marianna Misiura, b. 28 November 1819
Franciszka Misiura, b. 25 January 1823, d. 6 March 1892[13]

## FAMILY C-3

**Jan Chryzostom Skóra** was born to Michał Skóra and Jadwiga (Kramarz) Skóra on 23 January 1787 in Glinik and died there on 24 July 1847.[14] He married **Katarzyna Dziedzic** on 29 January 1816 in Glinik.[15] She was born to Wawrzyniec Dziedzic and Katarzyna (Mucha) Dziedzic on 16 November 1795 in Glinik and died there on 27 March 1832.[16]

Known children of Jan Chryzostom Skóra and Katarzyna (Dziedzic) Skóra, all born in Glinik:[17]

Marianna Skóra, b. 6 September 1818, d. 1 November 1822
Wojciech Skóra, b. 31 March 1820, d. 3 November 1822
Tomasz Skóra, b. 6 December 1821, d. 3 November 1822
Szymon Skóra, b. 16 October 1823, d. 26 April 1885 [Family C-5]
Marianna Skóra, b. 17 April 1826
Józef Skóra, b. 16 November 1829, d. 6 February 1851

The couple's first three children died within days of each other, almost certainly the victims of the same disease.

Five years after his wife Katarzyna's death, Jan Chryzostom married second Marianna (Cabaj) Ptaszek, a widow, on 14 November 1837 in Glinik; they had at least two children.[18]

## FAMILY C-4

**Wawrzyniec Cabaj** was born to Kazimierz Cabaj and Zofia (Litak) Cabaj on 3 August 1807 in Glinik and died there on 20 July 1855.[19] He married **Rozalia "Róża" Misiura** on 4 February 1834 in Glinik.[20] She was born to Michał Misiura and Agnieszka (Mytych) Misiura on 6 August 1816 in Glinik and died after 13 February 1856.[21]

Known children of Wawrzyniec Cabaj and Rozalia "Róża" (Misiura) Cabaj, all born in Glinik:[22]

Andrzej Cabaj, b. 10 November 1835, d. 1 March 1837
Andrzej Cabaj, b. 26 November 1837, d. 26 November 1901
[Family C-6]
Marianna Cabaj, b. 1 May 1840, d. 28 July 1855
Jan Cabaj, b. 13 May 1843, d. 1 June 1843
Jan Cabaj, b. 13 March 1846, d. 23 March 1846
Józef Cabaj, b. 23 February 1847
Antoni Cabaj, b. 5 March 1850, d. 23 July 1855
Marianna Cabaj, b. 13 February 1856

Only three of Wawrzyniec and Rozalia's children survived to adulthood.

Wawrzyniec himself died on 20 July 1855, followed by his five-year-old son Antoni on the 23rd and fifteen-year-old daughter Marianna on the 28th. It seems likely that they were victims of the same disease.

## FAMILY C-5

**Szymon Skóra** was born to Jan Chryzostom Skóra and Katarzyna (Dziedzic) Skóra on 16 October 1823 in Glinik and died there on 26 April 1885.[23] He married **Anna Mądro** about 1857.[24] She was born probably no later than about 1837 and died after 22 May 1880.[25]

Known children of Szymon Skóra and Anna (Mądro) Skóra, all born in Glinik:[26]

Józef Skóra, b. 3 February 1858, d. 25 February 1858
Józef Skóra, b. 19 August 1859
Wojciech Skóra, b. 17 April 1862
Antoni Skóra, b. 18 May 1864, d. 23 May 1864
Marianna Skóra, b. 26 July 1865, d. 19 December 1895 [Family C-6]
Helena Skóra, b. 24 April 1869
Jan Skóra, b. 30 April 1872
Stanisław Skóra, b. 23 April 1875
Antoni Skóra, b. 22 May 1880

## FAMILY C-6

**Andrzej Cabaj** was born to Wawrzyniec Cabaj and Rozalia (Misiura) Cabaj on 26 November 1837 in Glinik and died there on 26 November 1901.[27] He married first Marianna Kramarz with whom he had at least seven known children, including Józef and Wojciech (see p. 33).[28] He married second **Marianna Skóra** on 18 June 1888 in Łączki Kucharskie parish.[29] She was born to Szymon Skóra and Anna (Mądro) Skóra on 26 July 1865 in Glinik and died there on 19 December 1895.[30]

Known children of Andrzej Cabaj and Marianna (Skóra) Cabaj, all born in Glinik:[31]

Władysław "Walter" Cabaj, b. 18 July 1889, d. 27 June 1976
[Family C-7]
Katarzyna Cabaj, b. 27 March 1891[32]
Helena Cabaj, b. 18 January 1893
Józef Cabaj, b. 1 March 1895

After Marianna (Skóra) Cabaj's death, Andrzej married third Pryska Mądro; they he had at least two known children, both of whom died young.[33]

Entry for the marriage of Andrzej Cabaj and Marianna Skóra, 18 June 1888, in the Łączki Kucharskie parish register book.

*Glinik*

| Nrus serialis | 188 9 Dies et mensis Nat. Bap. | Nrus domus | Nomen BAPTISATI | Religio | | Sexus | | | PARENTES | | PATRINI Eorum | |
|---|---|---|---|---|---|---|---|---|---|---|---|---|
| | | | | Catholica | Acatholica | Puer | Puella | Thori | Patris ac parentum nomen cognomen et conditio ejus | Matris ac parentum nomen cognomen et conditio | Nomen et cognomen | Conditio |
| 9 | Julius | 1 | | | | 1 | | 1 | Gabriel Ku... | Agatha fil... A...l...... Pza | Franc... ... | |
| 31 | 18 21 88 Sept... July... | 88 | Ladis-laus | | | 1 | | ... | Andrzej Cabaj fil Lau-... et Rosalia M... ...jura ... Awie...w... ... | ...l s... Kwa... Ania di..... ... | Ava ...l... Schura Bzulla ...r Ava ...za ... | ... ... |

Entry for the birth and baptism of Władysław Cabaj, b. 18 July 1889, bap. 21 July 1889, in the Łączki Kucharskie parish register book.

# The Szymaszek Family in Poland

Peter Cabay's maternal ancestors (Szymaszek) came from several villages about five miles northeast of Dębica in what is now Dębica County, Podkarpackie Province, Poland. These include Lubzina, Paszczyna, and Wola Brzeźnicka, all within three miles of each other. Paszczyna lies eight miles north of Glinik and the two ancestral villages share the Wielopolka River. The land is given over mostly to farm fields.

The Szymaszek surname appears in available records dating to the turn of the nineteenth century.[34] The family name Szymaszek derives from the personal name Szymon (Simon).[35]

The available index records (*Poland, Church Books, 1568–1990*) are not consistent in giving the places of birth, marriage, and death events; for example, some alternate Lubzina and Paszczyna for events of members of the same household. There was no Roman Catholic church in Paszczyna, therefore, it seems likely that children known to have been born into Paszczyna households would have been baptized at the parish church in Lubzina.[36]

## FAMILY S-1

**Wojciech Szymaszek** was born about 1750 and died on 4 June 1813 in Paszczyna.[37] He married **Teresa Jedynak** on 21 September 1788 in Lubzina parish.[38] She was born to Maciej Jedynak and Zofia (-----) Jedynak in Paszczyna, baptized on 29 August 1768 in Lubzina, and died on 26 May 1845 in Paszczyna.[39]

Known children of Wojciech Szymaszek and Teresa (Jedynak) Szymaszek, all probably born in Paszczyna and baptized in Lubzina:

Andrzej Szymaszek, bap. 2 November 1789[40]

Marianna Szymaszek, bap. 25 February 1791[41]
Małgorzata Szymaszek, bap. 19 June 1792, d. 25 February 1794[42]
Teresa Szymaszek, bap. 2 September 1794[43]
Regina Szymaszek, bap. 16 March 1796[44]
Józef Szymaszek, bap. 8 March 1798[45]
Stanisław Szymaszek, bap. 4 May 1799[46]
Jan Szymaszek, bap. 6 June 1802[47]
Joanna Szymaszek, bap. 22 May 1803[48]
Antoni Szymaszek, bap. 26 May 1806[49]
Piotr Szymaszek, bap. 1 August 1807, d. 19 April 1868 [Family S-2]

After her husband Wojciech's death, Teresa married second Józef Gaweł on 25 November 1816 in Paszczyna.[50]

## FAMILY S-2

**Piotr Szymaszek** was baptized on 1 August 1807 in Lubzina parish, the son of Wojciech Szymaszek and Teresa (Jedynak) Szymaszek, and died on 19 April 1868 in Paszczyna.[51] He married **Katarzyna Grzegorski** on 11 January 1846 in Lubzina parish.[52] She was born to Błażej Grzegorski and Marianna (Czubczyński) Grzegorski about 1825 or 1826 and died on 18 December 1896 probably in Lubzina parish.[53]

Entry for the marriage of Piotr Szymaszek and Katarzyna Grzegorski, 11 January 1846, in the Lubzina parish register book.

Known children of Piotr Szymaszek and Katarzyna (Grzegorski) Szymaszek, all probably born in Paszczyna and baptized in Lubzina:

Andrzej Szymaszek, bap. 17 November 1846, d. 7 July 1847[54]
Wincenty Szymaszek, b. about 1848, d. 9 March 1850[55]
Marianna Szymaszek, bap. 8 April 1850, d. probably 9 August 1930[56]
Wiktoria Szymaszek, bap. 28 July 1852, d. probably 30 March 1937[57]
Jan Szymaszek, bap. 25 January 1855, d. 18 April 1909 [Family S-4]
Karolina Szymaszek, b. 7 April 1857[58]
Kunegunda Szymaszek, b. 16 June 1859, d. 11 March 1937[59]
Wincenty Szymaszek, b. 4 January 1862[60]
Antoni Szymaszek, b. 13 July 1865, d. 4 May 1868[61]

## FAMILY S-3

**Michał Strzok** was born to Wojciech Strzok and Katarzyna (Polniaszek) Strzok about 1800 or 1801 probably in or near Wola Brzeźnicka and died after 13 July 1851.[62] He married first Agata Mróz with whom he had at least eight known children.[63] He married second **Marianna (Paruch) Kusibab** on 13 July 1851 in Wola Brzeźnicka; she was the widow of Maciej Kusibab with whom she had at least two known children.[64] She was born to Bartłomiej Paruch and Katarzyna (Żurek) Paruch on 31 January 1814 in Pustków and died after 23 March 1852.[65]

Known child of Michał Strzok and Marianna (Paruch) Strzok, born in Wola Brzeźnicka:[66]

Franciszka Strzok, b. 23 March 1852, d. 1 August 1928 [Family S-4]

## FAMILY S-4

**Jan Szymaszek** was baptized on 25 January 1855 in Lubzina parish, the son of Piotr Szymaszek and Katarzyna (Grzegorski) Szymaszek, and died on 18 April 1909 probably in or near Paszczyna.[67] He married **Franciszka Strzok** on 24 October 1877 in Wola Brzeźnicka.[68] She was born to Michał Strzok and Marianna (Paruch) Strzok on 23 March 1852 in Wola Brzeźnicka and died on 1 August 1928 in Paszczyna.[69]

Known children of Jan Szymaszek and Franciszka (Strzok) Szymaszek, all probably born in or near Paszczyna:

Bronisława Szymaszek, b. 4 February 1880, d. 8 December 1881[70]

Weronika "Veronica" Szymaszek, b. 10 May 1882, d. 3 February 1957[71]

Marianna "Mary" Szymaszek, b. 9 February 1885, d. 12 October 1960[72]

Piotr "Peter" Szymaszek, b. 26 July 1887, buried 2 October 1945[73]

Stanisław Szymaszek, b. 20 April 1890, d. 1941[74]

Leokadia "Eleanore" Szymaszek, b. 13 February 1893, d. 25 February 1974 [Family C-7]

Honorata Szymaszek, b. 29 May 1898, d. 1985[75]

№ I 88/28
Zabrała

1/10 28 r. 9    Liczba czynności **A** 293/28

## Akt zejścia

spisany dnia _października 1928 w ..._

1. Imię i nazwisko zmarłego(ej) — (u kobiet zamężnych także nazwisko rodowe):
   _Franciszka Szymaszek ze Strzoków_

2. Zatrudnienie: _gospodyni_    _Rub B - lat 50_
   _Feb. 18?, 1839_
   _Łozn._

3. Wiek: _lat 80_

4. Wyznanie: _rzym-kat_

5. Stan (wolny, żonaty, zamężna, wdowiec, ~~wdowa~~, sądownie rozdzielony(a):

6. Gmina przynależności, obywatelstwo: _Paszczyna_

7. Stałe miejsce zamieszkania, adres mieszkania: _Paszczyna_
   (Jeśli zmarły pozostawał pod opieką lub kuratelą, należy wymienić sąd, który
   sprawował opiekę (kuratelę) i dołączyć dekret opiekuna (kuratora):

8. Dzień i miejsce skonu: _1 sierpnia 1928 w Paszczynie_

9. Pozostały małżonek (małżonka):

10. Pełnoletnie dzieci i pełnoletnie potomstwo zmarłych dzieci (imię i nazwisko, stan
    wiek i miejsce pobytu):
    1) _Weronika z Szymaszków Kurer lat 46 w Ameryce_
    2) _Marja z Szymaszków Rachwał lat 43 — "_
    3) _Piotr Szymaszek lat 40 w Ameryce_
    4) _Stanisław Szymaszek lat 33 w Paszczynie_
    5) _Leokadja z Szymaszków Łabaj lat 37 w Ameryce_
    6) _Honorata Szymaszek lat 30 w Paszczynie_

Form. № 4 post. niesp. (Akt zejścia).
Druk. Dz. Pr. W. K. Warszawa Długa 52. 1824-27.

The first page of the inheritance case file for Franciszka (Strzok) Szymaszek (1928) names her six living children and notes that four are in America and two are in Paszczyna.

Red Star Line
antwerpen - New York

S. S. Vaderland, June 20th 1905

Walter Cabaj came to the United States aboard the Red Star Line ship *Vaderland*.

Hamburg - Amerika Linie

Doppelschrauben-Postdampfer „Amerika"

Eleanore Szymaszek came to the United States aboard the Hamburg America Line ship *Amerika*.

# From Poland to Detroit

In early 1908, at age eighteen, Władysław Cabaj made his way from Austrian Poland to Antwerp, Belgium, where he boarded the ship *Vaderland* to cross the Atlantic Ocean. Eleven days later, on 11 February, he was processed at Ellis Island. Described as a laborer and carrying $20 (equivalent to $700 in 2024) to start a new life, his destination was Olyphant, Pennsylvania, where his half-brother Wojciech Cabaj lived.[76]

Wojciech—a son of Władysław's father Andrzej and his first wife, Marianna Kramarz—had come to the United States in 1905, settling near his full brother Józef who lived in Olyphant and worked in the nearby coal mines.[77] Sadly, Wojciech died in a mine roof fall accident in November 1909, one of 134 Polish miners in Pennsylvania who suffered the same fate that year.[78] This may have contributed to Władysław's decision to leave behind the coal mines and move to Detroit.

In 1912, Władysław first appears—under the name Walter Cabaj—in the Detroit city directory listed as a laborer boarding at 76 Greusel Avenue.[79] Also living at that address was Frank Rachwal and his wife Marianna "Mary" (Szymaszek) Rachwal.[80] It is not clear from records if the Cabaj family, the Rachwal family, and the Szymaszek family knew each other before arriving in the United States but it is possible, if not probable, given that they all lived within ten miles of each other in Poland. Nonetheless, Walter's future bride arrived at the house in May of that year.

"Walter" Cabaj in the 1912 Detroit city directory.

33

Leokadia Szymaszek arrived at Ellis Island on 12 May 1912 on the ship *Amerika*, her name being recorded as Eleanora (though most later documents have Eleanore). She was a nineteen-year-old farm laborer carrying $25 (equivalent to $815 in 2024), bound for her sister's and brother-in-law's home at 76 Greusel Avenue in Detroit.[81] (A note of historical interest: One month before Eleanore sailed on *Amerika*, the ship's crew had observed icebergs while crossing the North Atlantic and transmitted a warning about them which was received and relayed by *Titanic*. A similar message had also been sent that day to *Titanic* from *Baltic*, the ship John Joseph Quinn had sailed on in 1904. In fact, *Titanic* received numerous ice reports—apparently all unheeded—in the hours leading up to its infamous sinking.[82])

On 28 July 1913, Walter and Eleanore were married by Father Eustace Bartoszewicz at St. Hedwig Church in Detroit.[83] At the time of the 1920 census, they had two children and still resided on Greusel Avenue, splitting a home with Frank and Mary Rachwal and their six children.[84] Walter was employed as a foundry molder while Eleanore managed the household.[85]

A decade later, in April 1930, the family had grown to include five children. The Rachwals had moved to a farm north of the city and a new family shared the Greusel Avenue house—now numbered 3720 due to the 1921 Detroit street renumbering.[86] Walter was listed as an auto machine shop laborer. On 22 August, Walter took the first step toward obtaining citizenship by filing a Declaration of Intention. Five years later, on 29 April 1935, his citizenship petition was granted.[87] Around this time, the family bought a house and relocated to 6890 Ashton Avenue in the Warrendale neighborhood of Detroit.[88]

> ". . . three of us slept in one bed. We had just a living room, kitchen, and one bedroom, and a commode but no bath. . . . For the holidays you'd just get an orange or a sucker or something. . . . Mom used to sew dresses for us from bags of seed . . . and we survived. . . . [We were] a family that stuck together."[89]
>
> *Cecelia Cabay on growing up during the Great Depression*

Walter and Eleanore Cabaj on their wedding day, 28 July 1913. In the traditional Polish custom, Walter wears his wedding band on his right hand.

TRIPLICATE

# UNITED STATES OF AMERICA

No. 101471

## DECLARATION OF INTENTION

### (Invalid for all purposes seven years after the date hereof)

Eastern District of Michigan

Southern Division } ss:

In the _____ District _____ Court

of the United States at Detroit, Mich.

I, _____ Wladyslaw Cabaj _____
(Full true name, without abbreviation, and any other name which has been used, must appear here)

now residing at _____ 3720 Greusel, Detroit, Wayne Michigan _____
(Number and street) (City or town) (County) (State)

occupation _____ laborer _____, aged _____ 41 _____ years, do declare on oath that my personal description is:

Sex _____ male _____, color _____ white _____, complexion _____ fair _____, color of eyes _____ hazel _____

color of hair _____ brown _____, height _____ 5 _____ feet _____ 8 _____ inches; weight _____ 170 _____ pounds; visible distinctive marks

_____ none _____

race _____ Polish _____; nationality _____ Polish _____

I was born in _____ Glinik, Poland _____, on _____ July 25, 1888 _____
(City or town) (Country) (Month) (Day) (Year)

I am _____ married. The name of my wife or husband is _____ Eleonora _____

we were married on _____ June 13, 1913 _____, at _____ Detroit, Mich. _____; she or he was
(Month) (Day) (Year) (State or country)

born at _____ Paszczyna, Poland _____, on _____ Jan. 2, 1894 _____, entered the United States
(City or town) (State or country) (Month) (Day) (Year)

at _____ New York, N.Y. _____, on _____ May 11, 1912 _____, for permanent residence therein, and now
(City or town) (State) (Month) (Day) (Year)

resides at _____ Detroit, Mich. _____ I have _____ 5 _____ children, and the name, date and place of birth,
(State or country)

and place of residence of each of said children are as follows: Joseph, Dec. 7, 1915; Clara Aug. 26,
1919; Cecilia, Jan 26, 1922; Mary May 25, 1925; Peter, June 29, 1927
all born in Detroit, and now living with me.

I have _____ not _____ heretofore made a declaration of intention: Number _____, on _____

at _____, (Date)
(City or town) (State)

my last foreign residence was _____ Glinik, _____ Poland _____
(City or town) (Name of court) (Country)

I emigrated to the United States of America from _____ Bremen, _____ Germany _____
(City or town) (Country)

my lawful entry for permanent residence in the United States was at _____ New York, New York. _____
(City or town) (State)

under the name of _____ Wladislaw, Cabaj _____, on _____ Feb. 11, 1908 _____
(Month) (Day) (Year)

on the vessel _____ SS Vaderland _____
(If other than by vessel, state manner of arrival)

I will, before being admitted to citizenship, renounce forever all allegiance and fidelity to any foreign prince, potentate, state, or sovereignty, and particularly, by name, to the prince, potentate, state, or sovereignty of which I may be at the time of admission a citizen or subject; I am not an anarchist; I am not a polygamist nor a believer in the practice of polygamy; and it is my intention in good faith to become a citizen of the United States of America and to reside permanently therein; and I certify that the photograph affixed to the duplicate and triplicate hereof is a likeness of me: So HELP ME GOD.

*Wladyslaw Cabaj*
(Original signature of declarant without abbreviation, also alias, if used)

Subscribed and sworn to before me in the office of the Clerk of said Court,

at _____ Detroit, Mich. _____ this _____ 22d. _____ day of _____ August _____

anno Domini 19____ Certification No _____ 8-23573 _____ from the Commissioner of Naturalization showing the lawful entry of the declarant for permanent residence on the date stated above, has been received by me. The photograph affixed to the duplicate and triplicate hereof is a likeness of the declarant.

[SEAL]

_____ Deputy Clerk of the _____ Court.

By _____, Deputy Clerk.

Form 2202-L-A.

**U. S. DEPARTMENT OF LABOR**
NATURALIZATION SERVICE

14—2623 U. S. GOVERNMENT PRINTING OFFICE: 1930

The first page of Walter Cabaj's declaration of intention for citizenship, 1930.

The first half of the 1940s was a time of sacrifice for families around the world. Walter, now in his 50s, registered for the so-called "Old Man's Draft" (an inventory of manpower to be used toward the war effort) in April 1942.[90] As an employee of the Ford Rouge Plant he was a witness to and participant in the massive factory's shift to wartime production of tanks and other crucial war materiel. Walter and Eleanore's 21-year-old daughter Cecelia enlisted as an Army nurse at the beginning of 1944, eventually rising to the rank of First Lieutenant, Army Nurse Corps.[91] Their son Peter enlisted in the Marine Corps in October 1945.

By the 1950s, most of Walter and Eleanore's children had married and their grandchildren began to arrive, calling them *dziadziu* and *babchi*.[92] Eleanore's citizenship petition was granted on 20 January 1953.[93] The immigrant dream was fulfilled: safe passage, steady employment, citizenship, a growing family. Walter retired from a long career at Ford and continued to enjoy tending his garden while Eleanore expected everyone to be at Sunday dinner to savor her homemade noodles.[94] At Christmas, the family participated in sharing the *opłatek* (wafer) and this tradition is carried on today.[95]

Eleanore died on 25 February 1974 and Walter followed on 27 June 1976. They were buried at St. Hedwig Cemetery in Dearborn Heights, Wayne County, Michigan.[96]

## FAMILY C-7

**Władysław "Walter" Cabaj** was born to Andrzej Cabaj and Marianna (Skóra) Cabaj on 18 July 1889 in Glinik and died on 27 June 1976 in Detroit.[97] He married **Leokadia "Eleanore" Szymaszek** on 28 July 1913 in Detroit.[98] She was born to Jan Szymaszek and Franciszka (Strzok) Szymaszek on 13 February 1893 in Paszczyna and died on 25 February 1974 in Detroit.[99]

Known children of Władysław "Walter" Cabaj and Leokadia "Eleanore" (Szymaszek) Cabaj, all born in Detroit:[100]

Joseph Anthony "Joe" Cabaj, b. 7 December 1915, d. 17 June 2003[101]
Alphonse Cabaj, b. September 1917, d. May 1918[102]

Clara Theresa Cabaj/Cabay, b. 24 August 1919, d. 1 April 1994[103]

Cecelia Helen "Celia" Cabaj/Cabay, b. 26 January 1922, d. 20 May 2016[104]

Mary Magdalene Cabaj/Cabay, b. 25 May 1925, d. 21 April 1992[105]

Peter Paul "Pete" Cabaj/Cabay, b. 29 June 1927, d. 1 February 1999 [Family C-8]

Bernard Cabaj, b. 30 March 1929, d. 15 April 1929[106]

Eugene John "Gene" Cabaj, b. 27 December 1930, d. 14 June 2009[107]

# Background: Ireland

Dorothy Lucille Quinn was the daughter of John Joseph Quinn and Mary Gilligan, both immigrants from Ireland. John and Mary were born in the late 1800s into a country that had been under the control of England—and later, Great Britain—for centuries. The native Irish were portrayed as primitive and suffered from rampant oppression ranging from prohibitions on their language, music, fashion, and even haircuts. Most of the island's population lived in extreme poverty.[108] A growing independence movement was derailed by the Famine of 1845–1849. Over 1.3 million people died and another 1.4 million emigrated during this period.[109]

The Famine set in motion a huge wave of emigration from Ireland which continued until the first half of the twentieth century. By 1930, 4.5 million Irish had arrived in the United States.[110] John Quinn and Mary Gilligan were among the last of the wave of young Irish to leave their homeland seeking jobs—often menial or dangerous—and opportunities for better lives.

An evicted Irish family in the 1850s (Erskine Nicol, *An Ejected Family*).

# The Quinn and Gilligan Families in Ireland

Dorothy Quinn's paternal ancestors came from the area surrounding Ballina in County Mayo, Ireland, particularly the townland of Ardoughan. Ballina is situated on the River Moy in a plain of moorland and pastureland with mountains to the east and west and the Atlantic Ocean just seven miles to the north.

The Quinn surname is found in counties Clare, Longford, Mayo, and in Ulster. It is an Anglicized form of the Gaelic *Ó Coinn* ("descendant of Conn," *Conn* meaning "chief" or "wisdom").[111]

Dorothy's maternal ancestors (Gilligan) came from west central County Offaly (also known as King's County), particularly the townland of Lumcloon in Gallen parish near Ferbane. Located just a few miles east of the River Shannon, the area is dominated by lowland and bogs.

The Gilligan surname is found in counties Sligo, Offaly, and Roscommon. It is an Anglicized form of the Gaelic *Mac Giollagáin*, itself a diminutive of *giolla* meaning "lad."[112]

## FAMILY Q-1

**Thomas Quinn** was born to Terence Quinn and Anna (Brislow) Quinn between about 1840 and 1847 probably in Ardoughan and died there on 25 June 1924.[113] He married **Anne Hunter** on 1 December 1878 in Ballina.[114] She was born to James Hunter and Bridget (Gallagher) Hunter on 9 August 1855 probably in Ardoughan and died there on 31 December 1927.[115] Thomas and Anne were buried at Leigue Cemetery, Kilmoremoy, County Mayo.[116]

Known children of Thomas Quinn and Anne (Hunter) Quinn, all born in Ardoughan:

Mary Ellen Quinn, b. 24 April 1880[117]
John Joseph Quinn, b. 1 August 1882, d. 2 July 1962 [Family Q-2]
Margaret Quinn, b. 26 September 1884[118]
Thomas Quinn, b. 15 May 1886[119]
Anne Quinn, b. 2 January 1888[120]
Ellen Quinn, b. 29 March 1891[121]
Patrick James Quinn, b. 17 February 1893, d. July 1962[122]
Agnes Quinn, b. about 1895[123]
Lizzie Quinn, b. 10 December 1897[124]
Michael Thomas Quinn, b. 31 August 1900[125]

At the 1911 census, Thomas and Anne reported that they had twelve children, eight of whom were still living.[126]

Entry for the birth of John Joseph Quinn, 1 August 1882, in the Kilmoremoy parish register book (last line).

## FAMILY G-1

**James Gilligan** was born to Thomas Gilligan and Bridget (Kenny) Gilligan about 1803 or 1804 probably in Lumcloon and died there on 23 September 1879.[127] He married **Mary O'Brien** before about 1848.[128] She was born about 1820 or 1821 and died on 10 June 1875 in Lumcloon.[129] They had children including Bridget, Maria, and John [Family G-2].[130]

At the time of Griffith's valuation of property, published in 1854,

42

James leased from the Earl of Rosse just over nineteen acres of land with a house and outbuilding in Lumcloon townland. At the same time, he shared with Denis Gilligan—possibly his brother—a lease of three parcels totaling just over thirty-one acres in nearby Noggusduff townland.[131]

FAMILY G-2

**John Gilligan** was born to James Gilligan and Mary (O'Brien) Gilligan about 1851 probably in Lumcloon and died there on 13 March 1920.[132] He married **Anne Guinan** on 18 January 1887 in Cloghan.[133] She was born to Hugh Guinan and Bridget (Dolan) Guinan on 10 August 1867 in Lumcloon and died there on 3 June 1950.[134] John and Anne were buried at Kilrehan Cemetery, Kincora, County Offaly.[135]

Known children of John Gilligan and Anne (Guinan) Gilligan, all born in Lumcloon:[136]

Mary Gilligan, b. 28 September 1890, d. 31 May 1991 [Family Q-2]
James Gilligan, b. 2 August 1896[137]
Bridget Gilligan, b. 24 July 1902[138]
Margaret Gilligan, b. 10 March 1905[139]
Lucy Gilligan, b. 24 June 1907[140]

John Quinn came to the United States aboard the White Star Line ship *Baltic*.

Mary Gilligan came to the United States aboard the White Star Line ship *Arabic*.

# From Ireland to Detroit

At the 1901 census of Ireland, John Joseph Quinn lived with his widowed grandmother Bridget Hunter and two uncles and an aunt; all of them spoke English and Irish (Gaelic).[141] Presumably, his own family's home nearby was too crowded with two adults and six children.[142] Given the widespread poverty in Ireland, John—like millions of Irish people before him—decided to emigrate to the United States.

In September 1904, at age twenty-two, John made his way from County Mayo in the west of Ireland to Queenstown (now Cobh) near Cork in the south where he boarded the ship *Baltic* to come to the United States. On 30 September, he was processed at Ellis Island. Described as a laborer and carrying $10 (equivalent to $350 in 2024) to start a new life, his destination was Scranton, Pennsylvania, where his cousin Mary Hunter lived.[143] Mary worked as a "domestic" (maid) living at 1702 Wyoming Avenue in Scranton.[144] No records have been found to elucidate John's whereabouts from his arrival in the United States to his first appearance in Detroit in the 1913 city directory in which he is listed as a woodworker living at 119 Church Street (now 1833 or 1839 Church Street).[145]

Mary Gilligan was almost eighteen when she arrived at Ellis Island on the ship *Arabic* on 12 September 1908, having traveled the same route from Queenstown as her future husband John had four years earlier. She was listed as a servant, carrying $25 (equivalent to $700 in 2024), and bound for Rochester, New York, where her aunt Margaret Guinan lived.[146]

By 1910, Mary and her aunt Margaret lived and worked as domestic servants in the home of Frank Gebbie, his wife, adult daughter, and sister-in-law in Rochester.[147] The Gebbie family had become wealthy owing to Frank's business ventures including founding the Mohawk Condensed Milk Company.[148] However, sometime in the next two and a half years, Mary moved to Detroit.

On 11 March 1913, John and Mary were married by Father Ernest Van Dyke at St. Aloysius Church in Detroit.[149] On 27 June 1918, John took the first step toward obtaining citizenship by filing a Declaration of Intention.[150] At the time of the 1920 census, the couple had five children and rented a house in the Corktown neighborhood of Detroit at 228 Twelfth Street (now 1732 Rosa Parks Boulevard). John was employed as a foreman in the carpentry shop at Fisher Body Plant No. 10 (at the intersection of Dequindre and Theodore streets in Detroit) while Mary managed the household.[151]

By July 1923, the family had moved to 293 Avalon Avenue in Highland Park.[152] At the time of the 1930 census, there were ten children in the house and John had become a naturalized citizen.[153]

The family had once again moved by April 1935 and were renting at 10054 Holmur Street, Detroit. At the time of the 1940 census, the four oldest children had moved out leaving six at home. John was working as a watchman for Fisher Body, earning $2,000 per year (equivalent to $44,800 in 2024).[154] In 1942, John registered for the "Old Man's Draft" reporting an address of 5581 Ridgewood, Detroit.[155]

As a consequence of the financial burden of supporting ten children the family moved house frequently until settling into their Ridgewood home in the early 1940s. By 1950, only daughter Dorothy and son James still lived at home and both worked (as did John, now aged sixty-seven).[156]

John died on 2 July 1962. Mary lived to become a centenarian, dying on 31 May 1991, the grandmother of twenty-five, great-grandmother of sixty-three, and great-great-grandmother of ten.[157] They were buried at Holy Sepulchre Catholic Cemetery in Southfield, Oakland County, Michigan.[158]

John and Mary Quinn at daughter Dorothy's wedding, 1950.

**John Joseph Quinn** was born to Thomas Quinn and Anne (Hunter) Quinn about 2 August 1882 in Ardoughan and died on 2 July 1962 in Huron Township, Wayne County, Michigan.[159] He married **Mary Gilligan** on 11 March 1913 in Detroit.[160] She was born to John Gilligan and Anne (Guinan) Gilligan on 28 September 1890 in Lumcloon and died on 31 May 1991 in West Bloomfield Township, Oakland County, Michigan.[161]

Known children of John Joseph Quinn and Mary (Gilligan) Quinn, all born in Wayne County, Michigan:

Anne Marie Quinn, b. 3 June 1913, d. 14 September 1994[162]
Margaret Cecelia Quinn, b. 3 October 1914, d. 18 August 2001[163]
Thomas James Quinn, b. 19 February 1916, d. 27 March 1993[164]
Helen Agnes Quinn, b. 22 January 1918, d. 12 May 1997[165]
John Joseph "Jack" Quinn, Jr., b. 16 August 1919, d. 10 September 1996[166]
Catherine E. "Kay" Quinn, b. 13 August 1921, d. 17 May 1979[167]
William Quinn, b. 7 July 1923, d. 10 July 1923[168]
Joseph Michael "Joe" Quinn, b. 17 July 1924, d. 9 September 1986[169]
Agnes Elizabeth Quinn, b. 17 October 1925, d. 19 April 2000[170]
Dorothy Lucille Quinn, b. 25 March 1927, d. 7 September 2010 [Family C-8]
James Francis "Jim" Quinn, b. 18 November 1928, d. 16 December 1992[171]

Dorothy Cabay (L) and Agnes Daley (R) with their mother Mary Quinn at Dorothy's daughter Mary's wedding, 1986.

# Peter and Dorothy and Their Descendants

Peter Paul "Pete" Cabaj was born on 29 June 1927 in Detroit to Walter Cabaj and Eleanore (Szymaszek) Cabaj. A few years after his birth, the family moved from Greusel Avenue to Ashton Avenue where Pete and his siblings were raised.[172] The family attended Sts. Peter and Paul Church where Pete served as an altar boy.[173] He graduated from Mackenzie High School in June 1944.[174]

On his eighteenth birthday in 1945, Pete registered for the draft as required by law. At the time, he was employed at Cadillac Clark Street, Detroit.[175] With the war officially over but the country still under a national emergency, Pete chose to serve by enlisting in the United States Marine Corps on 5 Oct 1945. He spent a few weeks at Marine Corps Recruit Depot Parris Island, South Carolina, before receiving an honorable discharge on medical grounds.[176]

Pete enrolled in the University of Michigan's College of Engineering for the spring term of 1946, continuing his studies via extension correspondence the following academic year, and ending with the fall 1947 semester.[177] He did not complete a degree due to cost.[178] By 1949, Pete worked full time as a stenographer for an insurance company in downtown Detroit.[179] It was during this time that he met his future wife, Dorothy Lucille Quinn, who worked for another insurance company.[180]

Dorothy Lucille Quinn was born on 25 March 1927 in Detroit, the sixth daughter and tenth of eleven children of John Joseph Quinn and Mary (Gilligan) Quinn. She grew up in Detroit and attended St. Cecilia School.[181]

Pete and Dorothy were married on 7 October 1950 by Father James A. Machak at St. Cecilia Church in Detroit.[182] Around this time, Pete began to spell his surname as "Cabay" rather than "Cabaj."[183] After marriage, the couple lived with Pete's parents on Ashton Avenue and then moved a few blocks away to 6905 Rutland Street.[184] Their first child, a son named Peter was born in September 1951 but died shortly after birth. A daughter, Susan Eileen, was born a year later.

Pete and Dorothy Cabay on their wedding day, 7 October 1950.

In 1953, the family moved to 9376 Dixie, Redford.[185] Daughter Mary Margaret was born at the end of 1954. A son, Timothy Paul, was born in March 1960 but died at just two months old. Pete and Dorothy's third daughter, Catherine Theresa, was born in 1961.

Like their parents and grandparents before them, Pete and Dorothy both were brought up in the Roman Catholic church and they raised their daughters in the same tradition. The family attended Our Lady of Grace Church in Dearborn Heights where Susan, Mary, and Catherine attended elementary school. They then attended Bishop Borgess High School in Redford.[186] In 1978, Peter, Dorothy, and Catherine moved to 200 N. Ely Drive, Northville.[187] They attended Our Lady of Victory Church there.[188]

Pete and Dorothy traveled to Bermuda and Jamaica and visited Dorothy's parents' homeland and relatives in Ireland. They enjoyed dinner and dancing with friends, playing cards, and long drives together. Dorothy expressed her artistic skills with painting; Pete enjoyed golfing and—like his father—loved tending to his garden. Pete spent his working career in various roles in the automotive industry, eventually retiring from a Chrysler dealership in the late 1990s.[189]

Pete died on 1 February 1999 and Dorothy followed on 7 September 2010. They were buried at St. Hedwig Cemetery in Dearborn Heights, Wayne County, Michigan.[190]

Pete and Dorothy, 1990s.

Pete and Dorothy at the Hilton Hotel, Ocho Rios, Jamaica, 1963.

Pete and Dorothy at daughter Susan's wedding, 1977.

**Peter Paul "Pete" Cabaj/Cabay** was born to Władysław "Walter" Cabaj and Leokadia "Eleanore" (Szymaszek) Cabaj on 29 June 1927 in Detroit and died on 1 February 1999 in Livonia, Wayne County, Michigan.[191] He married **Dorothy Lucille Quinn** on 7 October 1950 in Detroit.[192] She was born to John Joseph Quinn and Mary (Gilligan) Quinn on 25 March 1927 in Detroit and died on 7 September 2010 in West Bloomfield Township, Oakland County, Michigan.[193]

Children, grandchildren, and great-grandchildren of Peter Paul "Pete" Cabay and Dorothy Lucille (Quinn) Cabay:[194]

1. Peter Cabay, Jr., b. and d. 19 September 1951[195]

2. Susan Eileen "Sue" Cabay, b. 1952
   + James Joseph "Jim" Delmotte, b. 1951
   *Married 21 May 1977, Bloomfield Hills, Michigan*

   a. Joseph Cabay "Joe" Delmotte, b. 1982
   + Vanessa Nicole Mitchell, b. 1983
   *Married 28 August 2010, San Diego, California*

   i. Jackson Patrick "Jack" Delmotte, b. 2014
   ii. Mason James Delmotte, b. 2014
   iii. Liv Sue Delmotte, b. 2018

   b. Emily Catherine Delmotte, b. 1986
   + Christopher Duane "Chris" Cook, b. 1982
   *Married 19 August 2017, Ann Arbor, Michigan*

   i. Aidan James Cook, b. 2020
   ii. Lily Susannah Cook, b. 2024

   c. Rachel Elizabeth Delmotte, b. 1988

3. Mary Margaret Cabay, b. 1954
   + Eugene Theodore "Gene"/"Ted" Parent, b. 6 November
     1932, d. 15 September 2006[196]
   *Married 6 April 1986, Independence Township, Michigan*

      a. Timothy Cabay "Tim" Parent, b. 1988
      + Alyssa Danielle Wilson, b. 1987
      *Married 14 December 2024, W. Bloomfield Twp., Mich.*

   + David Robert "Dave" Moore, b. 1954
   *Married 23 November 2012, Rochester Hills, Michigan*


4. Timothy Paul Cabay, b. 7 March 1960, d. 21 May 1960[197]


5. Catherine Theresa "Cathy" Cabay, b. 26 May 1961,
   d. 31 December 2015[198]
   + Eric Boyd Black, b. 1959
   *Married 26 June 1993, Novi, Michigan*

      a. Tyler Cabay Black, b. 1994
      b. Peter Quinn Black, b. 1997

# Abbreviated Citations

These abbreviated citations are used to indicate certain sources in the Endnotes and Illustration Credits which follow.

**FSL DGS**

FamilySearch Library Digital Filming Numbers.

These numbers can be searched in the FamilySearch Library online catalog to retrieve specific groups of digitized resources (https://familysearch.org/search/catalog). Some resources can only be viewed onsite at a FamilySearch Center or affiliated library.

**Geneteka**

Polskie Towarzystwo Genealogiczne. Geneteka: Genealogiczna kartoteka - baza urodzeń, małżeństw i zgonów. https://geneteka.genealodzy.pl.

[Polish Genealogical Society. Geneteka: Genealogical Records - Database of Births, Marriages, and Deaths].

**Interviews**

Interviews with Susan Eileen (Cabay) Delmotte, Mary Margaret (Cabay) Moore, and Emily Catherine Delmotte by Christopher D. Cook, conducted in 2024 and 2025.

**_Ireland, Birth and Baptism, 1763–1917_**

*Ireland, Select Catholic Birth and Baptism Registers, 1763–1917.* Ancestry.com. https://www.ancestry.com/search/collections/6068.

"This collection includes Catholic baptismal registers from 73 parishes in Ireland, with dates ranging from 1763 to 1912 (noninclusive; coverage will vary by parish). Children were typically baptized soon after they were born. The details found in baptismal registers vary but can include: name, baptismal date, father's name, mother's name, godparents'/sponsors' names, place."

## Ireland, Civil Records

Ireland. Department of Tourism, Culture, Arts, Gaeltacht, Sport and Media. IrishGenealogy.ie. Civil Records. https://www.irishgenealogy.ie.

## *Ireland, Death and Burial, 1767–1992*

*Ireland, Select Catholic Death and Burial Registers, 1767–1992*. Ancestry.com. https://www.ancestry.com/search/collections/9055.

"This collection includes Catholic death and burial registers from 19 parishes in Ireland, with dates ranging from 1767 to 1992 (noninclusive; coverage will vary by parish). The details found in burial registers vary but can include: name of the deceased, age, date of death, burial date."

Note: as of this writing, the records for Ballina, County Mayo, 1907–1932, are incorrectly described as being from County Tipperary; the content of the records, however, is evidently from Ballina, County Mayo.

## Kurcz

Kurcz, John Jerome ("Jerry"). "The Szymaszek Family." Updated 1 May 2019. Unpublished typescript. Copy in the collection of Susan Eileen (Cabay) Delmotte.

Jerry Kurcz's history of the Szymaszek family is informative and useful as a starting point for further research. Unfortunately, he did not provided source citations and his facts, therefore, cannot be verified easily. Information given from Kurcz in this book should not be assumed to be correct; it is provided here for the sake of completeness and showing previous genealogical work.

## ŁKP Księgi małżeństw, M-345

Catholic Church, Łączki Kucharskie Parish (Ropczyce, Podkarpackie, Poland). "Księgi małżeństw [Marriage record books], 1815–1834, 1837–1854." United M-345 (FSL DGS 8004152, images 452–757 of 757).

## ŁKP Księgi urodzeń, M-343

Catholic Church, Łączki Kucharskie Parish (Ropczyce, Podkarpackie, Poland). "Księgi urodzeń [Birth record books], 1815–1834, 1837–1840." Unit M-343 (FSL DGS 8004152, images 5–247 of 757).

## ŁKP Księgi urodzeń, M-344

Catholic Church, Łączki Kucharskie Parish (Ropczyce, Podkarpackie, Poland). "Księgi urodzeń [Birth record books], 1841–1854." Unit M-344 (FSL DGS 8004152, images 269–440 of 757).

## ŁKP Księgi zgonów, M-346

Catholic Church, Łączki Kucharskie Parish (Ropczyce, Podkarpackie, Poland). "Księgi zgonów [Death record books], 1815–1834, 1837–1854." Unit M-346 (FSL DGS 7997516).

## *Poland, Church Books, 1568–1990*

*Poland, Church Books, 1568–1990.* FamilySearch. https://www.familysearch.org/en/search/collection/4135958.

"Indexes of church books containing baptisms and births, marriages, burials and deaths. Records are from various parishes of the Greek Catholic Church, Roman Catholic Church and Evangelical Church."

# Endnotes

1. Wikipedia, "Polish name," last modified 20 August 2025, 03:53 (UTC), https://en.wikipedia.org/wiki/Polish_name.

2. "The Nation of Polonia," *Immigration and Relocation in U.S. History*, Library of Congress, https://www.loc.gov/classroom-materials/immigration/polish-russian/the-nation-of-polonia.

3. Geneteka, birth, marriage, and death entries for Cabaj, search parameters: province: Podkarpackie, parish: all locations, person surname: Cabaj.

4. "Cabaj," Internetowy słownik nazwisk w Polsce [Internet Dictionary of Surnames in Poland], Instytut Języka Polskiego, Polskiej Akademii Nauk, 2022, https://nazwiska.ijppan.pl/haslo/show/name/CABAJ.

5. Geneteka, entry for birth of Kazimierz Cabaj, 1781, record 11, search parameters: province: Podkarpackie, parish: Łączki Kucharskie, person surname: Cabaj, person name: Kazimierz (gives place, house number [80], birthdate, and parents' names).
   ŁKP Księgi zgonów, M-346, p. 499, no. 14, death record of Kazimierz Cabaj, 9 March 1850 (FSL DGS 7997516, image 286 of 369).

6. Geneteka, entry for marriage of Kazimierz Cabaj and Zofia Litak, 1806, record 2, search parameters: province: Podkarpackie, parish: Łączki Kucharskie, person surname: Cabaj, person name: Kazimierz, or person surname: Litak, or person name: Zofia (gives place and date of marriage).

7. Geneteka, entry for birth of Zofia Litak, 1785, record 10, search parameters: province: Podkarpackie, parish: Łączki Kucharskie, person surname: Litak, person name: Zofia (gives place, house number [94], birthdate, and parents' names).
   Geneteka, entry for death of Zofia Cabaj, 1857, record 19, search parameters: province: Podkarpackie, parish: Łączki Kucharskie, person surname: Cabaj, person name: Zofia, or person surname: Litak (gives place, age [72], deceased husband's name, and date of death).

8. Geneteka, birth and death entries for children of Kazimierz Cabaj and Zofia Litak, search parameters: province: Podkarpackie, parish: Łączki Kucharskie, person surname: Cabaj, person name: Kazimierz, or person surname: Litak, or person name: Zofia.

9. Birth year calculated from age (76) at death; ŁKP Księgi zgonów, M-346, p. 275, death record of Michał Misiura, 15 November 1838 (FSL DGS 7997516, image 174 of 369).

10. Geneteka, entry for marriage of Michał Misiura and Agnieszka Mytych, 1801, record 12, search parameters: province: Podkarpackie, parish: Łączki Kucharskie, person surname: Misiura, person name: Michał, or person surname: Mytych, or person name: Agnieszka (gives place and date of marriage).

11. ŁKP Księgi zgonów, M-346, p. 214, no. 13, death record of Agnieszka (Mytych) Misiura, 4 April 1844 (FSL DGS 7997516, image 214 of 369).

12. Geneteka, birth entries for children of Michał Misiura and Agnieszka Mytych, search parameters: province: Podkarpackie, parish: Łączki Kucharskie, person surname: Misiura, person name: Michał, or person surname: Mytych, or person name: Agnieszka.

13. Geneteka, entry for birth of Franciszka Misiura, 1823, record 37, search parameters: province: Podkarpackie, parish: Łączki Kucharskie, person surname: Misiura, person name: Michał, or person surname: Mytych (gives place, birthdate, and parents' names with mother as "Agata," probably in error, rather than "Agnieszka").

   Geneteka, entry for marriage of Jakub Pociask and Franciszka Misiura, 1839, record 17, search parameters: province: Podkarpackie, parish: Łączki Kucharskie, person surname: Misiura, person name: Franciszka, or person surname: Mytych (gives Franciszka's parents' names as Michał Misiura and Agnieszka Mytych).

   Geneteka, entry for death of Franciszka Pociask, 1892, record 10, search parameters: province: Podkarpackie, parish: Łączki Kucharskie, person surname: Misiura, person name: Franciszka, or person surname: Mytych (gives place, maiden name, birth year, deceased husband's name, house number [153], date of death, and parents' names with mother as "Agata").

14. Geneteka, entry for birth of Jan Chryzostom Skóra, 1787, record 2, search parameters: province: Podkarpackie, parish: Łączki Kucharskie, person surname: Skóra, person name: Jan Chryzostom (gives place, house number [116], birthdate, and parents' names).

   ŁKP Księgi zgonów, M-346, p. [416], no. 69, death record of Jan Chryzostom Skóra, 24 July 1847 (FSL DGS 7997516, image 245 of 369).

15. ŁKP Księgi małżeństw, M-345, p. 15, no. 1, marriage record of Jan Skóra and Katarzyna Dziedzic (FSL DGS 8004152, image 460 of 757).

16. Geneteka, entry for birth of Katarzyna Dziedzic, 1795, record 33, search parameters: province: Podkarpackie, parish: Łączki Kucharskie, person surname: Dziedzic, person name: Katarzyna (gives place, house number [29], birthdate, and parents' names).

   ŁKP Księgi zgonów, M-346, p. 235, death record of Katarzyna Skóra, 27 March 1832 (FSL DGS 7997516, image 154 of 369).

17. Geneteka, birth and death entries for children of Jan Skóra and Katarzyna Dziedzic, search parameters: province: Podkarpackie, parish: Łączki Kucharskie, person surname: Skóra, person name: Jan, or person surname: Dziedzic, or person name: Katarzyna.

18. ŁKP Księgi małżeństw, M-345, p. 221, marriage record of Jan Skóra and

Marianna (Cabaj) Ptaszek (FSL DGS 8004152, image 563 of 757). The records currently available to me do not elucidate this Marianna Cabaj's place in the Cabaj family tree.

Geneteka, birth entries for children of Jan Skóra and Marianna Cabaj, search parameters: province: Podkarpackie, parish: Łączki Kucharskie, person surname: Skóra, person name: Jan, or person surname: Cabaj, or person name: Marianna, range of years: from 1837 to 1849.

19. Geneteka, entry for birth of Wawrzyniec Cabaj, 1807, record 21, search parameters: province: Podkarpackie, parish: Łączki Kucharskie, person surname: Cabaj, person name: Wawrzyniec (gives place, house number [40], birthdate, and parents' names).

Geneteka, entry for death of Wawrzyniec Cabaj, 1855, record 48, search parameters: province: Podkarpackie, parish: Łączki Kucharskie, person surname: Cabaj, person name: Wawrzyniec (gives place, age [43, should be 47], wife's name, and date of death).

20. ŁKP Księgi małżeństw, M-345, p. [218], marriage record of Wawrzyniec Cabaj and Rozalia Misiura (FSL DGS 8004152, image 562 of 757).

Rozalia's name is recorded as "Róża" in her birth record and the birth record of her last child with Wawrzyniec and as "Rozalia" in their marriage record and the available birth and death records of their other children.

21. ŁKP Księgi urodzeń, M-343, p. [30], no. 16 [bis], birth record of Róża Misiura (FSL DGS 8004152, image 20 of 757).

No death record for Rozalia "Róża" (Misiura) Cabaj located.

22. Geneteka, birth and death entries for children of Wawrzyniec Cabaj and Rozalia Misiura, search parameters: province: Podkarpackie, parish: Łączki Kucharskie, person surname: Cabaj, person name: Wawrzyniec, or person surname: Misiura, or person name: Roza.

An unnamed girl was stillborn on 11 March 1854; ŁKP Księgi zgonów, M-346, p. 623, no. 22, death record of unnamed girl Cabaj, 11 March 1854 (FSL DGS 7997516, image 348 of 369).

23. ŁKP Księgi urodzeń, M-343, p. 178, no. 34, birth record of Szymon Skóra (FSL DGS 8004152, image 94 of 757).

Geneteka, entry for death of Szymon Skóra, 1885, record 16, search parameters: province: Podkarpackie, parish: Łączki Kucharskie, person surname: Skóra, person name: Szymon (gives place, date of death, and age [62, should be 61]).

24. Marriage year estimated from birth of first known child.

25. Birth year estimated at about age 21 at marriage; no birth or death records for Anna (Mądro) Skóra located.

26. Geneteka, birth and death entries for children of Szymon Skóra and Anna Mądro, search parameters: province: Podkarpackie, parish: Łączki Kucharskie, person surname: Skóra, person name: Szymon, or person surname: Mądro.

27. ŁKP Księgi urodzeń, M-343, p. [390], birth record of Andrzej Cabaj (FSL

DGS 8004152, image 201 of 757).

Geneteka, entry for death of Andrzej Cabaj, 1901, record 31, search parameters: province: Podkarpackie, parish: Łączki Kucharskie, person surname: Cabaj, person name: Andrzej (gives place, birth year, house number [88], date of death, parents' names, and notes that Andrzej was the widower of Marianna Kramarz and Marianna Skóra and husband of Pryska Mądro).

28. Geneteka, birth and death entries for children of Andrzej Cabaj and Marianna Kramarz, search parameters: province: Podkarpackie, parish: Łączki Kucharskie, person surname: Cabaj, person name: Andrzej, or person surname: Kramarz.

29. Catholic Church, Łączki Kucharskie Parish (Ropczyce, Podkarpackie, Poland), *Księgi metrykalne parafii rzymskokatolickiej Łączki Kucharskie [Parish Register Books of the Roman Catholic Parish of Łączki Kucharskie]*, Małżeństwa [Marriages], p. 649, no. 3, marriage record of Andrzej Cabaj and Marianna Skóra, 18 June 1888: digital image at: Skanoteka – Metryki: Baza skanów akt metrykalnych [Database of Scans of Vital Records], Collection: 11094, Unit: 1888 / UMZ-1888, Unit Description: Marriages, File: 002, https://metryki.genealodzy.pl/id3312-sy1888-kt2.

30. Geneteka, entry for birth of Marianna Skóra, 1865, record 30, search parameters: province: Podkarpackie, parish: Łączki Kucharskie, person surname: Skóra, person name: Marianna (gives place, house number [116], birthdate, and parents' names).

Geneteka, entry for death of Marianna Cabaj, 1895, record 62, search parameters: province: Podkarpackie, parish: Łączki Kucharskie, person surname: Cabaj, person name: Marianna, or person surname: Skóra (gives place, maiden name, birth year, husband's name, house number [88], date of death, and parents' names).

31. Geneteka, birth entries for children of Andrzej Cabaj and Marianna Skóra, search parameters: province: Podkarpackie, parish: Łączki Kucharskie, person surname: Cabaj, person name: Andrzej, or person surname: Skóra, range of years: from 1888.

32. On 9 July 1910, a marriage license was issued to Antoni Wojcik and a Katarzyna Cabaj—age 19, born in Austria, and with parents "Andrew" and "Maryany"—in Wayne County, Michigan, however the marriage was not performed (Wayne County, Michigan, *Marriage Records, 1836–1913; Index 1836–1937*, Marriages, v. 15 (1910), p. 181, no. 72109, entry for Antoni Wojcik and Katharzyna [*sic*] Cabaj, 9 July 1910 [FSL DGS 4255417, image 187 of 720]). I have been unable to positively identify this person in other documents or trace her further.

33. Geneteka, entry for marriage Andrzej Cabaj and Pryska Mądro, 1896, record 5, search parameters: province: Podkarpackie, parish: Łączki Kucharskie, person surname: Cabaj, person name: Andrzej, or person surname: Mądro, or person name: Pryska (gives place, his birth year, her birth year [1864], date of marriage, his parents' names, her mother's name, and notes he is the widow

of Marianna Skóra).

Geneteka, birth and death entries for children of Andrzej Cabaj and Pryska Mądro, search parameters: province: Podkarpackie, parish: Łączki Kucharskie, person surname: Cabaj, person name: Andrzej, or person surname: Mądro, or person name: Pryska.

34. *Poland, Church Books, 1568–1990*, "Szymaszek," https://www.familysearch.org/en/search/collection/4135958.

35. "Szymaszek," Internetowy słownik nazwisk w Polsce [Internet Dictionary of Surnames in Poland], Instytut Języka Polskiego, Polskiej Akademii Nauk, 2022, https://nazwiska.ijppan.pl/haslo/show/name/SZYMASZEK.

36. "Historia parafii," Parafia Lubzina, https://parafialubzina.pl/historia.

37. Birth year estimated from age (40) at marriage and age (60) at death.
    *Poland, Church Books, 1568–1990*, "Adalbertus Szymaszek, Death," https://www.familysearch.org/ark:/61903/1:1:6VQG-9423.

38. *Poland, Church Books, 1568–1990*, "Adalbertus Szymaszek, Marriage," https://www.familysearch.org/ark:/61903/1:1:6VQG-GBB8.

39. *Poland, Church Books, 1568–1990*, "Theressiam Jedynak, Baptism," https://www.familysearch.org/ark:/61903/1:1:6VQJ-X2BJ.
    *Poland, Church Books, 1568–1990*, "Theresia Jedynakowna, Death," https://www.familysearch.org/ark:/61903/1:1:6VQF-1B36.

40. *Poland, Church Books, 1568–1990*, "Andreas Szymaszek, Baptism," https://www.familysearch.org/ark:/61903/1:1:6VQK-WWGF.

41. *Poland, Church Books, 1568–1990*, "Marianna Szymaszek, Baptism," https://www.familysearch.org/ark:/61903/1:1:6VQK-D9V6.

42. *Poland, Church Books, 1568–1990*, "Margaritha Szymaszek, Baptism," https://www.familysearch.org/ark:/61903/1:1:6VQK-GQL7.
    *Poland, Church Books, 1568–1990*, "Margaritha Symaszek [*sic*], Death," https://www.familysearch.org/ark:/61903/1:1:6VQK-PRRF.

43. *Poland, Church Books, 1568–1990*, "Theressa Szymaszek, Baptism," https://www.familysearch.org/ark:/61903/1:1:6VQV-YTXN.

44. *Poland, Church Books, 1568–1990*, "Regina Szymaszek, Baptism," https://www.familysearch.org/ark:/61903/1:1:6VQK-Q6P9.

45. *Poland, Church Books, 1568–1990*, "Josephus Szymaszek, Baptism," https://www.familysearch.org/ark:/61903/1:1:6VQV-1PFX.

46. *Poland, Church Books, 1568–1990*, "Stanisl Szymaszek, Baptism," https://www.familysearch.org/ark:/61903/1:1:6VQK-HX8G.

47. *Poland, Church Books, 1568–1990*, "Joannes Szymaszek, Baptism," https://www.familysearch.org/ark:/61903/1:1:6VQK-6QB1.

48. *Poland, Church Books, 1568–1990*, "Joann Szymaszek, Baptism," https://www.familysearch.org/ark:/61903/1:1:6VQK-HXPJ.

49. *Poland, Church Books, 1568–1990*, "Antonius Szymaszek, Baptism," https://www.familysearch.org/ark:/61903/1:1:6VQV-TPXV.

50. *Poland, Church Books, 1568–1990*, "Josephus Gawel, Marriage," https://www.familysearch.org/ark:/61903/1:1:6VQG-R63M.

51. *Poland, Church Books, 1568–1990*, "Petrus Szymaszek, Baptism," https://www.familysearch.org/ark:/61903/1:1:6VQK-Q6W3.
    *Poland, Church Books, 1568–1990*, "Petrus Szymaszek, Death," https://www.familysearch.org/ark:/61903/1:1:6VQN-QCLW.

52. *Poland, Church Books, 1568–1990*, "Petrus Szymaszek, Marriage," https://www.familysearch.org/ark:/61903/1:1:6VQ9-YX7X.

53. Birth year estimated from age (19) at marriage.
    *Poland, Church Books, 1568–1990*, "Catharina Szymaszek Grzegorska, Death," https://www.familysearch.org/ark:/61903/1:1:6VQG-FNT5.

54. *Poland, Church Books, 1568–1990*, "Andraeas Szymaszek, Baptism," https://www.familysearch.org/ark:/61903/1:1:6VQ2-J6R9.
    *Poland, Church Books, 1568–1990*, "Andreas Szymaszek, Death," https://www.familysearch.org/ark:/61903/1:1:6VQ3-BMYK.

55. Birth year estimated from age (2) at death.
    *Poland, Church Books, 1568–1990*, "Vicentius Szymaszek, Death," https://www.familysearch.org/ark:/61903/1:1:6VQL-39G7.

56. *Poland, Church Books, 1568–1990*, "Marianna Szymaszek, Baptism," https://www.familysearch.org/ark:/61903/1:1:6VQ2-VVHN.
    Kurcz has her date of death but with no source.

57. *Poland, Church Books, 1568–1990*, "Victoria Szymanszek, Baptism," https://www.familysearch.org/ark:/61903/1:1:6VQK-S1YT.
    Kurcz has her date of death but with no source.

58. *Poland, Church Books, 1568–1990*, "Carolina Szymaszek, Baptism," https://www.familysearch.org/ark:/61903/1:1:6VQ2-BFQB (gives birthdate and date of baptism).

59. *Poland, Church Books, 1568–1990*, "Cunegundis Szymaszek, Baptism," https://www.familysearch.org/ark:/61903/1:1:6VQ2-VV7F (gives birthdate as 16 June 1859 and date of baptism as 19 June 1859); "Mrs. George Boro Dies," *Columbus Telegraph* (Columbus, Neb.), 12 March 1937, p. 8 (gives birthdate as 16 May 1859).

60. *Poland, Church Books, 1568–1990*, "Vincentius Szymaszek, Baptism," https://www.familysearch.org/ark:/61903/1:1:6VQL-9HFM (gives birthdate and date of baptism).

61. *Poland, Church Books, 1568–1990*, "Antonius Szymaszek, Baptism," https://www.familysearch.org/ark:/61903/1:1:6VQ2-LYYB (gives birthdate and date of baptism.)
    *Poland, Church Books, 1568–1990*, "Antonius Szymaszek, Death," https://www.familysearch.org/ark:/61903/1:1:6VQS-BMML.

62. Birth year estimated from age (24) at marriage to Agata Mróz and age (50) at marriage to Marianna (Paruch) Kusibab.
    Died after marriage to Marianna (Paruch) Kusibab.

63. Geneteka, entry for marriage of Michał Strzok and Agata Mróz, 1825, record 3, search parameters: province: Podkarpackie, parish: Brzeźnica, person surname: Strzok, person name: Michał (gives place, his age [24], her age [25],

house number [5], date of marriage, and parents' names).

    Geneteka, birth entries for children of Michał Strzok and Agata Mróz, search parameters: province: Podkarpackie, parish: Brzeźnica, person surname: Strzok, person name: Michał, or person surname: Mróz, or person name: Agata.

64.    Geneteka, entry for marriage of Michał Strzok and Marianna Kusibabowna, 1851, record 1, search parameters: province: Podkarpackie, parish: Brzeźnica, person surname: Strzok, person name: Michał, or person surname: Kusibabowna, or person name: Marianna (gives place, his age [50], her age [36], date of marriage, and notes he is a widower and she is a widow).

    Geneteka, entry for marriage of Maciej Kusibab and Marianna Paruch, 1833, record 1, search parameters: province: Podkarpackie, parish: Brzeźnica, person surname: Kusibab, person name: Maciej, or person surname: Paruch, or person name: Marianna.

    Geneteka, birth entries for children of Maciej Kusibab and Marianna Paruch, search parameters: province: Podkarpackie, parish: Brzeźnica, person surname: Kusibab, person name: Maciej, or person surname: Paruch, or person name: Marianna.

65.    Geneteka, entry for birth of Marianna Paruch, 1814, record 4, search parameters: province: Podkarpackie, parish: Brzeźnica, person surname: Paruch, person name: Marianna (gives place, house number [16], birthdate, and parents' names).

    Died after birth of daughter Franciszka.

66.    Geneteka, birth entry for child of Michał Strzok and Marianna Paruch, search parameters: province: Podkarpackie, parish: Brzeźnica, person surname: Strzok, person name: Michał, or person surname: Paruch, or person name: Marianna.

67.    *Poland, Church Books, 1568–1990*, "Joannes Szymanskzek [*sic*], Baptism," https://www.familysearch.org/ark:/61903/1:1:6VQL-MY23.

    *Poland, Church Books, 1568–1990*, "Joannes Szymaszek, Death," https://www.familysearch.org/ark:/61903/1:1:6VQJ-3FYL.

68.    Geneteka, entry for marriage of Jan Szymaszek and Franciszka Strzok, 1877, record 2, search parameters: province: Podkarpackie, parish: Brzeźnica, person surname: Szymaszek, person name: Jan, or person surname: Strzok, or person name: Franciszka (gives place, his age [22], her age [25], date of marriage, and parents' names).

69.    Geneteka, entry for birth of Franciszka Strzok, 1852, record 3, search parameters: province: Podkarpackie, parish: Brzeźnica, person surname: Strzok, person name: Franciszka (gives place, birthdate, and parents' names).

    *Poland, Church Books, 1568–1990*, "Francisca Szymaszek Slurok [*sic*], Death," https://www.familysearch.org/ark:/61903/1:1:6VQG-C8ST; Sąd Powiatowy w Dębicy [Dębica District Court], Akta sprawy spadkowej po Franciszce Szymaszek z Paszczyny, zmarłej 1 sierpnia 1928 [Inheritance Case Files of Franciszka Szymaszek of Paszczyna Who Died on 1 August 1928],

Archiwum Państwowe w Przemyślu [State Archives, Przemyśl, Poland], A293/28, digital copy in the collection of Christopher D. Cook.

70. *Poland, Church Books, 1568–1990*, "Bronislava Szymaszek, Baptism," https://www.familysearch.org/ark:/61903/1:1:6VQ2-GCZ1.

   *Poland, Church Books, 1568–1990*, "Bronislava Szymaszek, Death," https://www.familysearch.org/ark:/61903/1:1:6VQN-SX5P.

71. *Poland, Church Books, 1568–1990*, "Veronica Szypna [*sic*], Baptism," https://www.familysearch.org/ark:/61903/1:1:6VQ2-2TPP.

   "[Death Notice of Veronica Kurcz]," *Detroit Free Press*, 5 February 1957, p. 24 ("... age 74 ... sister of Mary Rachwal of Richmond, Mich., Mrs. Eleanor Cabaj of Detroit, and Honorata Rozak in Poland."); St. Hedwig Cemetery staff, email message to Christopher D. Cook, 29 April 2025 ("Veronica Kurcz ... DOD 2/3/1957").

72. *Poland, Church Books, 1568–1990*, "Marianna Szymaszek, Baptism," https://www.familysearch.org/ark:/61903/1:1:6VQ2-FC1P.

   Mary Rachwal memorial stone, St. Hedwig Cemetery, Dearborn Heights, Wayne County, Michigan, "Feb. 9, 1885 – Oct. 12, 1960".

73. U.S. District Court, Eastern District of Michigan, Southern Division, *Michigan, Wayne County, Naturalization Records, 1837–1999*, Naturalization Petitions and Records, v. 298, no. 73501–73750 (1932), Declaration of Intention of Peter Szymaszek, no. 177570, 1 September 1926, and Petition for Citizenship of Piotr Szymaszek, no. 73695, 20 January 1933 (FSL DGS 102164354, images 802–805 of 1033).

   Peter Szymaszek memorial stone, St. Hedwig Cemetery, Dearborn Heights, Wayne County, Michigan, "1887 – 1945"; St. Hedwig Cemetery staff, email message to Christopher D. Cook, 29 April 2025 ("burial date is 10/2/1945").

74. *Poland, Church Books, 1568–1990*, "Stanislaus Szymaszak [*sic*], Baptism," https://www.familysearch.org/ark:/61903/1:1:6VQ2-FZWX.

   Kurcz has his year of death as 1941 but with no source.

75. *Poland, Church Books, 1568–1990*, "Honoratha Szymaszek, Baptism," https://www.familysearch.org/ark:/61903/1:1:6VQK-CTXG.

   Kurcz has her year of death as 1985 but with no source.

76. *Passenger and Crew Lists of Vessels Arriving at New York, 1897–1942*, Passenger Manifest, Ship *Vaderland* (Antwerp to New York), arriving 11 February 1908, list 3, entry 28 for Władysław Cabaj (FSL DGS 7658636, images 54–55 of 970).

77. Geneteka, birth entries for children of Andrzej Cabaj and Marianna Kramarz, search parameters: province: Podkarpackie, parish: Łączki Kucharskie, person surname: Cabaj, person name: Andrzej, or person surname: Kramarz; *Passenger and Crew Lists of Vessels Arriving at New York, 1897–1942*, Passenger Manifest, Ship *Grosser Kurfürst* (Bremen to New York), arriving 5 April 1905, list 35, entry 9 for Wojciech Cabaj (FSL DGS 5262971, image 407 of 813).

78. Lackawanna County, Pennsylvania, Death Certificate of Wojciech Cabaj,

filed 4 November 1909; *Report of the Department of Mines of Pennsylvania, 1909* (Harrisburg: C. E. Aughinbaugh, Printer to the State of Pennsylvania, 1910), pt. 1, p. 27 and pt. 2, p. cxxxi.

79. *Detroit City Directory for the Year Commencing September 1st, 1912* (Detroit: R. L. Polk & Co., 1912), p. 766.

I have been unable to locate Władysław Cabaj in the 1910 census.

80. *Detroit City Directory for the Year Commencing September 1st, 1912* (Detroit: R. L. Polk & Co., 1912), p. 2080.

"Frank Rachwal [obituary]," *Times Herald* (Port Huron, Michigan), 18 July 1958, p. 8 (". . . married the former Mary Seymaszek [*sic*], 1907, in Detroit.").

Kurcz has Frank's origin as Okonin (which is halfway between Glinik and Paszczyna) but with no source. His birth name was almost certainly Franciszek Rachwał. I have been unable to locate his immigration records.

81. *Passenger and Crew Lists of Vessels Arriving at New York, 1897–1942*, Passenger Manifest, Ship *Amerika* (Hamburg to Southampton to Cherbourg to New York), arriving 12 May 1912, list 33, entry 26 for Eleanora [*sic*] Szymaszek (FSL DGS 7675885, images 224–225 of 819).

82. *"Titanic" Disaster: Report of the Committee on Commerce, United States Senate* (Washington: Government Printing Office, 1912), p. 6–7.

83. Wayne County, Michigan, *Marriage Records, 1836–1913; Index 1836–1937*, Marriages, v. 20 (1913), p. 59, no. 96485, entry for Wladyslaw Czabaj [*sic*] and Eleanore Szymaszek, 25 July 1913 (FSL DGS 4674396, image 420 of 744).

84. 1920 U.S. Census, Michigan, Wayne County, Detroit, E. D. 501, sheet 51B, family 264, household of Frank Rachwal, and family 265, household of Walter Cabon [i.e., Cabaj].

This census lists a Frank Cabon [i.e., Cabaj], age 26, born in Poland, arrived in the U.S. in 1913, as Walter's brother; I have been unable to positively identify this person's parentage or immigration records.

85. "Cecelia Cabay Collection," Veterans History Project, American Folklife Center, Library of Congress, https://www.loc.gov/item/afc2001001.94341 (". . . mom stayed home.").

86. 1930 U.S. Census, Michigan, Wayne County, Detroit, E. D. 82–498, sheet 1B, family 15, household of Walter Cabaij [*sic*].

"Frank Rachwal [obituary]," *Times Herald* (Port Huron, Michigan), 18 July 1958, p. 8.

87. U.S. District Court, Eastern District of Michigan, Southern Division, *Michigan, Wayne County, Naturalization Records, 1837–1999*, Naturalization petitions and records, v. 337, no. 83250–83500 (1934), records of Władysław Cabaj (FSL DGS 102198791, images 940–943 of 1125).

88. 1940 U.S. Census, Michigan, Wayne County, Detroit, E. D. 84–1641, sheet 1A, family 9, household of Walter Sabaj [i.e., Cabaj].

89. "Cecelia Cabay Collection," Veterans History Project, American Folklife

Center, Library of Congress, https://www.loc.gov/item/afc2001001.94341.

90. *Michigan Selective Service System Registration Cards [World War II]: Fourth Registration*, Walter Cabaj, 27 April 1942 (FSL DGS 4670080, image 3603 of 4940).

91. Entry for Cecelia H. Cabay, *The BIRLS Database*, Reclaim the Records, https://www.birls.org; "Cecelia Cabay Collection," Veterans History Project, American Folklife Center, Library of Congress, https://www.loc.gov/item/afc2001001.94341.

92. Interviews (S.E.D.).

93. U.S. District Court, Eastern District of Michigan, Southern Division, *Michigan, Wayne County, Naturalization Records, 1837–1999*, Naturalization petitions and records, v. 865, no. 237951– 238300 (1950–1953), records of Eleanore Cabaj (FSL DGS 102973712, images 1140–1142).

94. Interviews (S.E.D.).

95. Interviews (S.E.D.).

96. Walter Cabaj memorial stone, St. Hedwig Cemetery, Dearborn Heights, Wayne County, Michigan; Eleanore Cabaj memorial stone, St. Hedwig Cemetery, Dearborn Heights, Wayne County, Michigan.

97. Catholic Church, Łączki Kucharskie Parish (Ropczyce, Podkarpackie, Poland), *Księgi metrykalne parafii rzymskokatolickiej Łączki Kucharskie [Parish Register Books of the Roman Catholic Parish of Łączki Kucharskie]*, Urodzenia [Births], p. 841, no. 31, birth record of Władysław Cabaj, 18 July 1889: digital image at: Skanoteka – Metryki: Baza skanów akt metrykalnych [Database of Scans of Vital Records], Collection: 11094, Unit: 1889 / UMZ-1889, Unit Description: Births, Years: 1889, File: 012, https://metryki.genealodzy.pl/id3312-sy1889-kt1.

   Walter's birthdate and age vary throughout the sources. The earliest and most local to his birth, the Łączki Kucharskie/Glinik parish register cited above, gives his birthdate as 18 July 1889 with baptism on 21 July 1889. His age is correctly recorded in the *Vaderland* passenger manifest (18, 11 February 1908) and his marriage registration (24, 25 July 1913). On his naturalization forms (cited above) his birthdate is given as 25 July 1888.

   "[Death Notice of Walter Cabaj]," *Detroit Free Press*, 29 June 1976, p. 4-C.

98. Wayne County, Michigan, *Marriage Records, 1836–1913; Index 1836–1937*, Marriages, v. 20 (1913), p. 59, no. 96485, entry for Wladyslaw Czabaj [*sic*] and Eleanore Szymaszek, 25 July 1913 (FSL DGS 4674396, image 420 of 744).

99. *Poland, Church Books, 1568–1990*, "Leocadia Szymaszek, Baptism," https://www.familysearch.org/ark:/61903/1:1:6VQ2-K28H.

   Eleanore's birthdate and age vary throughout the sources. The earliest and most local to her birth, the Paszczyna parish register cited above, gives her birthdate as 13 February 1893 with baptism the next day. Her age is incorrectly recorded in the *Amerika* passenger manifest (20, 2 May 1912) but correctly a year later in her marriage registration (20, 25 July 1913). Her alien registration form (U.S. Immigration and Naturalization Service, Form AR-2, Alien Registration Form of Elenore [*sic*] Cabay, no. A1059964, 30 September 1940, National Archives and Records Administration) gives her birthdate as 2 January 1894 while her naturalization forms (cited above) and death certificate (cited below) give 4 February 1893.

Wayne County, Michigan, Death Certificate of Eleanore Cabaj, filed 27 February 1974.

100. There may have been two additional children who died young; "Cecelia Cabay Collection," Veterans History Project, American Folklife Center, Library of Congress, https://www.loc.gov/item/afc2001001.94341 ("There was ten children. Four died and six of us survived.").

101. Entry for Joseph Anthony Cabaj, Social Security no. 363030694, *Numerical Identification Files (NUMIDENT), Application (SS-5) Files, 1936–2007*, National Archives and Records Administration, http://aad.archives.gov/aad/series-description.jsp?s=5057; Entry for Joseph Anthony Cabaj, Social Security no. 363030694, *Numerical Identification Files (NUMIDENT), Death Files, 1936–2007*, National Archives and Records Administration, http://aad.archives.gov/aad/series-description.jsp?s=5057.

102. "Begräbnisscheine," *Detroiter Abend-Post* (Detroit), 23 May 1918, p. 7, col. 4.

103. Entry for Clara Theresa Cabay, Social Security no. 374142531, *Numerical Identification Files (NUMIDENT), Application (SS-5) Files, 1936–2007*, National Archives and Records Administration, http://aad.archives.gov/aad/series-description.jsp?s=5057; Macomb County, Michigan, Death Certificate of Clara Mangner, filed 1 April 1994.

104. Entry for Cecelia H. Cabay, *The BIRLS Database*, Reclaim the Records, https://www.birls.org; "Cecelia Cabay Collection," Veterans History Project, American Folklife Center, Library of Congress, https://www.loc.gov/item/afc2001001.94341.

105. Entry for Mary Magdalene Dombkowski, Social Security no. 376204045, *Numerical Identification Files (NUMIDENT), Application (SS-5) Files, 1936–2007*, National Archives and Records Administration, http://aad.archives.gov/aad/series-description.jsp?s=5057.

106. Wayne County, Michigan, Death Certificate of Bernard Cabaj, filed 16 April 1929.

107. Entry for Eugene John Cabaj, *The BIRLS Database*, Reclaim the Records, https://www.birls.org; "Cabaj, Eugene John [obituary]," *News Sentinel* (Knoxville, Tennessee), 17 June 2009, p. A12.

108. John O'Beirne Ranelagh, *A Short History of Ireland*, 3rd ed. (Cambridge: Cambridge University Press, 2012), p. 49, 57, and 123.

109. John O'Beirne Ranelagh, *A Short History of Ireland*, 3rd ed. (Cambridge: Cambridge University Press, 2012), p. 123–124.

110. "Irish-Catholic Immigration to America," *Immigration and Relocation in U.S. History*, Library of Congress, https://www.loc.gov/classroom-materials/immigration/irish/irish-catholic-immigration-to-america.

111. Patrick Hanks, Simon Lenarčič, and Peter McClure, eds., *Dictionary of Amer-*

*ican Family Names*, 2nd ed. (New York: Oxford University Press, 2022), s.v. Quinn.

112. Patrick Hanks, Simon Lenarčič, and Peter McClure, eds., *Dictionary of American Family Names*, 2nd ed. (New York: Oxford University Press, 2022), s.v. Gilligan.

113. Birth year estimated from age in censuses (cited below) in 1901 (54), 1911 (70), and at death (82).

    Church records have his death on 25 June 1924 and burial on 27 June 1924 while civil records have his death on 18 June 1924, almost certainly incorrectly: *Ireland, Death and Burial, 1767–1992*, county: Tipperary [*sic*], parish: Ballina, year range: 1907–1932, p. 188, no. 1108, death record of Thomas Quinn, 25 June 1924 (image 108 of 207); Ireland, Civil Records, Ballina Superintendent Registrar's District, Ballina Registrar's District, County Mayo, no. 30, death record of Thomas Quinn, 18 June 1924, registered 21 July 1924.

114. *Ireland, Select Catholic Marriage Registers, 1778–1942*, county: Mayo, parish: Ballina (Kilmoremoy), year range: 1868–1911, folio 37, no. 475, marriage record of Thomas Quinn and Anne Hunter, 1 December 1878 (images 78–79 of 229), Ancestry.com, https://www.ancestry.com/search/collections/9055.

    Ireland, Civil Records, Ballina Superintendent Registrar's District, Ballina Registrar's District, Counties of Mayo and Sligo, no. 137, marriage record of Thomas Quinn and Anne Hunter, 1 December 1878, registered 31 December 1878.

115. Catholic Church, Kilmoremoy Parish (Mayo and Sligo, Ireland), "Baptismal Register, Ardnaree, 1849–1868," p. 61, no. [897], baptism record of Anne Hunter, 9 August 1855 (FSL DGS 7732597, item 16, image 36 of 150).

    *Ireland, Death and Burial, 1767–1992*, county: Tipperary [*sic*], parish: Ballina, year range: 1907–1932, p. 233, no. 1372, death record of Anne Quinn, 31 December 1927 (image 153 of 207); Ireland, Civil Records, Ballina Superintendent Registrar's District, Ballina Registrar's District, County Mayo, no. 316, death record of Anne Quinn, 31 December 1927, registered 23 January 1928.

116. *Ireland, Death and Burial, 1767–1992*, county: Tipperary [*sic*], parish: Ballina, year range: 1907–1932, p. 188, no. 1108, death record of Thomas Quinn, 25 June 1924 (image 108 of 207); *Ireland, Death and Burial, 1767–1992*, county: Tipperary [*sic*], parish: Ballina, year range: 1907–1932, p. 233, no. 1372, death record of Anne Quinn, 31 December 1927 (image 153 of 207).

117. Ireland, Civil Records, Ballina Superintendent Registrar's District, Ballina Registrar's District, Counties of Mayo and Sligo, no. 362, birth record of Mary Ellen Quinn, 24 April 1880, registered 11 May 1880 (has father as "Terence Quinn" and mother as "Anne Quinn formerly ~~Brislow~~ Hunter" clearly mistaking Mary Ellen's grandparents' names for her parents).

118. Ireland, Civil Records, Ballina Superintendent Registrar's District, Ballina

Registrar's District, Counties of Mayo and Sligo, no. 456, birth record of Margaret Quinn, 26 September 1884, registered 14 November 1884.

119. Ireland, Civil Records, Ballina Superintendent Registrar's District, Ballina Registrar's District, Counties of Mayo and Sligo, no. 413, birth record of Thomas Quinn, 15 May 1886, registered 18 June 1886.

120. Ireland, Civil Records, Ballina Superintendent Registrar's District, Ballina Registrar's District, Counties of Mayo and Sligo, no. 473, birth record of Anne Quinn, 2 January 1888, registered 2 February 1888.

121. Ireland, Civil Records, Ballina Superintendent Registrar's District, Ballina Registrar's District, Counties of Mayo and Sligo, no. 152, birth record of Ellen Quinn, 29 March 1891, registered 12 June 1891.

122. Ireland, Civil Records, Ballina Superintendent Registrar's District, Ballina Registrar's District, Counties of Mayo and Sligo, no. 356, birth record of Patrick James Quinn, 17 February 1893, registered 28 March 1893; Entry for Patrick James Quinn, Social Security no. 714034901, *Numerical Identification Files (NUMIDENT), Application (SS-5) Files, 1936–2007*, National Archives and Records Administration, http://aad.archives.gov/aad/series-description. jsp?s=5057 (had birthdate as 7 February 1893); "New Jersey Death Index – 1962 – Surnames N–Z," Reclaim the Records, 17 July 2018, https://archive. org/details/NJ_Death_Index_1962_N-Z, entry for Patrick J. Quinn, file no. 34945; Patrick J. Quinn memorial stone, Mount Olivet Cemetery, Newark, Essex County, New Jersey.

123. Civil record of birth not found; listed on 1901 and 1911 censuses (cited below).

124. Ireland, Civil Records, Ballina Superintendent Registrar's District, Ballina Registrar's District, Counties of Mayo and Sligo, no. 126, birth record of Lizzie Quinn, 10 December 1897, registered 19 February 1898.

125. Ireland, Civil Records, Ballina Superintendent Registrar's District, Ballina Registrar's District, County Mayo, no. 490, birth record of Michael Thomas Quinn, 31 August 1900, registered 17 November 1900.

126. Census of Ireland, 1901, County Mayo, Ballina Poor Law Union, Ballina Rural Electoral Division District, Tirawley Barony, Kilmoremoy Parish, Ardoughan Townland, house no. 9, household of Thomas Quinn; Census of Ireland, 1911, County Mayo, Ballina Poor Law Union, Ballina Rural Electoral Division District, Tirawley Barony, Kilmoremoy Parish, Ardoughan Townland, house no. 5, household of Thomas Quinn.

127. Parents' names from Josh Guinan, email message to Christopher D. Cook, 26 May 2025, citing research of Margaret Koster and Margaret Williams, descendants of Bridget (Gilligan) Fitzgerald.

   Birth year estimated from age (75) at death.

   Ireland, Civil Records, Parsonstown Superintendent Registrar's District, Ferbane Registrar's District, King's County, no. 171, death record of James Gilligan, 23 September 1879, registered 25 November 1879.

128. Wife's name from Josh Guinan, email message to Christopher D. Cook, 26

May 2025, citing research of Margaret Koster and Margaret Williams, descendants of Bridget (Gilligan) Fitzgerald; marriage year estimated from age (17) of daughter Bridget upon her arrival in Australia in 1865 (see below).

129. Birth year estimated from age (54) at death.

Ireland, Civil Records, Parsonstown Superintendent Registrar's District, Ferbane Registrar's District, King's County, no. 176, death record of Mary Gilligan, 10 June 1875, registered 18 June 1875.

130. James and Mary's daughters Bridget and Maria emigrated to Australia in 1865 to live with their uncle, John Gilligan, in Parramatta, New South Wales; Bridget was 17 and Maria was 15 (Josh Guinan, email message to Christopher D. Cook, 26 May 2025, citing research of Margaret Koster and Margaret Williams, descendants of Bridget [Gilligan] Fitzgerald; *New South Wales, Australia, Assisted Immigrant Passenger Lists, 1828–1896*, year: 1865, month: March, vessel: *Himalaya*, folio 7 [bis], entry 38 for Bridget Gilligan and entry 39 for Maria Gilligan [image 20 of 32], Ancestry.com, https://www.ancestry.com/search/collections/1204).

131. Richard Griffith, *General Valuation of Rateable Property in Ireland: King's County: Valuation of the Several Tenements in the Union of Parsonstown Situate in the County above Named* (Dublin: Printed by Alexander Thom and Sons for Her Majesty's Stationery Office, 1854), p. 121, 123.

132. Birth year estimated from age (69) at death; his sister Maria likely was born in 1850 (see above).

Ireland, Civil Records, Birr Superintendent Registrar's District, Ferbane Registrar's District, King's County, no. 498, death record of John Gilligan, 13 March 1920, registered 24 March 1920.

133. Ireland, Civil Records, Parsonstown Superintendent Registrar's District, Banagher Registrar's District, King's County, no. 59, marriage record of John Gilligan and Anne Guinan, 18 January 1887.

134. Ireland, Civil Records, Parsonstown Superintendent Registrar's District, Ferbane Registrar's District, King's County, no. 212, birth record of Anne Guinan, 10 August 1867, registered 29 August 1867.

Ireland, Civil Records, Birr Superintendent Registrar's District, Ferbane District, County Offaly, no. 265, death record of Anne Gilligan, 3 June 1950, registered 6 June 1950.

135. John, Anne, Mary, and James Gilligan memorial stone, Kilrehan Cemetery, Kincora, County Offaly, Ireland.

136. Census of Ireland, 1911, King's County, Birr Poor Law Union, Gallen District Electoral Division, Garrycastle Barony, Gallen Parish, Lumcloon Townland, house no. 8, household of John Gilligan.

137. Ireland, Civil Records, Parsonstown Superintendent Registrar's District, Ferbane Registrar's District, King's County, no. 464, birth record of James Gilligan, 2 August 1896, registered 30 July 1897.

138. Ireland, Civil Records, Birr Superintendent Registrar's District, Ferbane Registrar's District, King's County, no. 37, birth record of Bridget Gilligan, 24

July 1902, registered 12 August 1902.

139. Ireland, Civil Records, Birr Superintendent Registrar's District, Ferbane Registrar's District, King's County, no. 300, birth record of Margaret Gilligan, 10 March 1905, registered 17 March 1905.

140. Ireland, Civil Records, Birr Superintendent Registrar's District, Ferbane Registrar's District, King's County, no. 75, birth record of Lucy Gilligan, 24 June 1907, registered 30 July 1907 (has mother as "Bridgid Gilligan formerly Guinan" in error).

141. Census of Ireland, 1901, County Mayo, Ballina Poor Law Union, Ballina Rural District Electoral Division, Tirawley Barony, Kilmoremoy Parish, Ardoughan Townland, house no. 2, household of Bridget Hunter.

142. Census of Ireland, 1901, County Mayo, Ballina Poor Law Union, Ballina Rural District Electoral Division, Tirawley Barony, Kilmoremoy Parish, Ardoughan Townland, house no. 9, household of Thomas Quinn.

143. *Passenger and Crew Lists of Vessels Arriving at New York, 1897–1942*, Passenger Manifest, Ship *Baltic* (Liverpool to Queenstown to New York), arriving 30 September 1904, list QU, entry 26 for John Quinn (FSL DGS 5262866, image 44 of 558).

144. *R. L. Polk & Co.'s Scranton Directory 1904* (Scranton, Pa.: R. L. Polk & Co., [1904]), p. 399.
    I have been unable to identify Mary Hunter or John Quinn in Scranton directories for adjacent years or in the 1910 census.

145. *Detroit City Directory for the Year Commencing September 1st, 1913* (Detroit: R. L. Polk & Co., 1913), p. 1765.

146. *Passenger and Crew Lists of Vessels Arriving at New York, 1897–1942*, Passenger Manifest, Ship *Arabic* (Liverpool to Queenstown to New York), arriving 12 September 1908, list 1, entry 4 for Mary Gilligan (FSL DGS 7658924, images 620–621 of 849).

147. 1910 U.S. Census, New York, Monroe County, Rochester, E. D. 77, sheet 5B, family 113, household of Frank Gebbie.

148. "Who We Are," Gebbie Foundation, https://www.gebbie.org/whoweare.

149. Wayne County, Michigan, *Marriage Records, 1836–1913; Index 1836–1937*, Marriages, v. 19 (1912–1913), p. 119, no. 92154, entry for John Quinn and Mary Gilligan, 11 Mar 1913 (FSL DGS 4674396, image 125 of 744).

150. U.S. District Court, Eastern District of Michigan, Southern Division, *Michigan, Wayne County, Naturalization Records, 1837–1999*, Naturalization Petitions and Records, v. 32, no. 14691–15190 (1918), Declaration of Intention of John Joseph Quinn, no. 14915, 27 June 1918 (FSL DGS 103501581, images 281 of 565).

151. 1920 U.S. Census, Michigan, Wayne County, Detroit, E. D. 238, sheet 8B, family 171, household of John Quinn; *World War I Selective Service System Draft Registration Cards, 1917–1918*, John Joseph Quinn, 12 September 1918 (FSL DGS 5257974, image 5459 of 6024); "The Night Shift," *Nailhed* (blog), spring 2014, https://www.nailhed.com/2014/06/the-night-shift.html.

152. Wayne County, Michigan, Death Certificate of William Quinn, filed 17 July 1923.

153. 1930 U.S. Census, Michigan, Wayne County, Highland Park, E. D. 82-979, sheet 28B, family 409, household of John Quinn.

154. 1940 U.S. Census, Michigan, Wayne County, Detroit, E. D. 84-818, sheet 7B, family 153, household of John Quinn.

155. *Michigan Selective Service System Registration Cards [World War II]: Fourth Registration*, John Joseph Quinn, 27 April 1942 (FSL DGS 4673201, image 3546 of 6118).

156. 1950 U.S. Census, Michigan, Wayne County, Detroit, E. D. 85-1547, sheet 4, family 42, household of John Quinn; Interviews (S.E.D.).

157. "[Death Notice of Mary Quinn]," *Detroit Free Press*, 1 June 1991, p. 9A.

158. John J. Quinn memorial stone, Holy Sepulchre Catholic Cemetery, Southfield, Oakland County, Michigan; Mary Quinn, memorial stone, Holy Sepulchre Catholic Cemetery, Southfield, Oakland County, Michigan.

159. *Ireland, Birth and Baptism, 1763–1917*, county: Mayo, parish: Ballina (Kilmoremoy), year range: 1879–1891, folio 55, no. 669, birth and baptism record of Joannes Joseph Quinn, 1 and 3 August 1882 (images 116–117 of 344).

John used 2 August as his birthdate on documents throughout his life, for example, his draft registrations and Declaration of Intention (all cited above). The record of his birth and baptism, written contemporaneously with the events, gives 1 August for his birth and 3 August for his baptism. I have been unable to locate a civil record of his birth.

Wayne County, Michigan, Death Certificate of John Joseph Quinn, filed 10 July 1962; "[Death Notice of John Joseph Quinn]," *Detroit Free Press*, 4 July 1962, p. B-7.

160. Wayne County, Michigan, *Marriage Records, 1836–1913; Index 1836–1937*, Marriages, v. 19 (1912–1913), p. 119, no. 92154, entry for John Quinn and Mary Gilligan, 11 March 1913 (FSL DGS 4674396, image 125 of 744).

161. Ireland, Civil Records, Parsonstown Superintendent Registrar's District, Ferbane Registrar's District, King's County, no. 127, birth record of Mary Gilligan, 28 September 1890, registered 17 October 1890.

Oakland County, Michigan, Death Certificate of Mary Quinn, filed 3 June 1991 (has errors including birthdate as 21 September 1890, father's name as Thomas, and mother's name as Bridget); "[Death Notice of Mary Quinn]," *Detroit Free Press*, 1 June 1991, p. 9A.

162. Entry for Anne Marie Sims, Social Security no. 375016519, *Numerical Identification Files (NUMIDENT), Application (SS-5) Files, 1936–2007*, National Archives and Records Administration, http://aad.archives.gov/aad/series-description.jsp?s=5057; Entry for Anne M. Sims, Social Security no. 375016519, *Numerical Identification Files (NUMIDENT), Death Files, 1936–2007*, National Archives and Records Administration, http://aad.archives.gov/aad/series-description.jsp?s=5057 (day of death not recorded,

cycle date 24 September 1994); "Sims, Anne M.," *Detroit Free Press*, 16 September 1994, p. 4B.

163. Entry for Margaret Cecelia Deyell, Social Security no. 364168967, *Numerical Identification Files (NUMIDENT), Application (SS-5) Files, 1936–2007*, National Archives and Records Administration, http://aad.archives.gov/aad/series-description.jsp?s=5057; Entry for Margaret C. Deyell, Social Security no. 364168967, *Numerical Identification Files (NUMIDENT), Death Files, 1936–2007*, National Archives and Records Administration, http://aad.archives.gov/aad/series-description.jsp?s=5057.

164. *Michigan, World War II Draft Registration Cards, 1940–1947*, Thomas James Quinn, 16 October 1940 (FSL DGS 105305871, image 106 of 1088); Entry for Thomas J. Quinn, Social Security no. 374095372, *Numerical Identification Files (NUMIDENT), Death Files, 1936–2007*, National Archives and Records Administration, http://aad.archives.gov/aad/series-description.jsp?s=5057.

165. Entry for Helen Agnes Walker, Social Security no. 366188110, *Numerical Identification Files (NUMIDENT), Application (SS-5) Files, 1936–2007*, National Archives and Records Administration, http://aad.archives.gov/aad/series-description.jsp?s=5057; Entry for Helen Agnes Walker, *Social Security no. 366188110, Numerical Identification Files (NUMIDENT), Death Files, 1936–2007*, National Archives and Records Administration, http://aad.archives.gov/aad/series-description.jsp?s=5057.

166. Entry for John Josph [*sic*] Quinn, Social Security no. 374072591, *Numerical Identification Files (NUMIDENT), Application (SS-5) Files, 1936–2007*, National Archives and Records Administration, http://aad.archives.gov/aad/series-description.jsp?s=5057; Entry for John J. Quinn, Social Security no. 374072591, *Numerical Identification Files (NUMIDENT), Death Files, 1936–2007*, National Archives and Records Administration, http://aad.archives.gov/aad/series-description.jsp?s=5057 (has birthdate as 15 August 1919).

167. Wayne County, Michigan, Death Certificate of Catherine E. Daley, filed 23 May 1979.

168. Wayne County, Michigan, Death Certificate of William Quinn, filed 17 July 1923.

169. *Michigan, World War II Draft Registration Cards, 1940–1947*, Joseph Michael Quinn, 30 December 1942 (FSL DGS 105305761, image 1083 of 1098); *Michigan, Death Index, 1971–1996*, FamilySearch, entry for Joseph M. Quinn, 9 Sep 1986, certificate no. 56693, https://www.familysearch.org/ark:/61903/1:1:VZ1D-DNJ.

170. Entry for Agnes Elizabeth Daley, Social Security no. 369201253, *Numerical Identification Files (NUMIDENT), Application (SS-5) Files, 1936–2007*, National Archives and Records Administration, http://aad.archives.gov/aad/series-description.jsp?s=5057; Entry for Agnes E. Daley, Social Security no. 369201253, *Numerical Identification Files (NUMIDENT), Death Files,*

*1936–2007*, National Archives and Records Administration, http://aad. archives.gov/aad/series-description.jsp?s=5057.

171. Entry for James Francis Quinn, Social Security no. 368306089, *Numerical Identification Files (NUMIDENT), Application (SS-5) Files, 1936–2007*, National Archives and Records Administration, http://aad.archives.gov/ aad/series-description.jsp?s=5057; Entry for James F. Quinn, Social Security no. 368306089, *Numerical Identification Files (NUMIDENT), Death Files, 1936–2007*, National Archives and Records Administration, http://aad. archives.gov/aad/series-description.jsp?s=5057.

172. 1940 U.S. Census, Michigan, Wayne County, Detroit, E. D. 84–1641, sheet 1A, family 9, household of Walter Sabaj [i.e., Cabaj].

173. Susan E. Delmotte, eulogy delivered at the funeral of Peter Paul Cabay, 5 February 1999, typescript in the collection of Susan Eileen (Cabay) Delmotte.

174. *Stag, June 1944* (Detroit: Mackenzie High School, 1944), p. 6.

175. *Michigan, World War II Draft Registration Cards, 1940–1947*, Peter Paul Cabaj, 29 June 1945 (FSL DGS 105305935, image 141 of 1078).

176. U.S. Marine Corps, Certificate of Discharge Under Honorable Conditions of Peter Paul Cabay, 27 October 1945, copy in the collection of Susan Eileen (Cabay) Delmotte.

177. *Register of Students, 1945–1946* (Ann Arbor: University of Michigan, n.d.), p. 65; *Register of Students, 1946–1947* (Ann Arbor: University of Michigan, n.d.), p. 74; *Register of Students, 1947–1948* (Ann Arbor: University of Michigan, n.d.), p. 70.

178. Interviews (S.E.D.).

179. 1950 U.S. Census, Michigan, Wayne County, Detroit, E. D. 85–2709, sheet 41, family 389, household of Walter Cabaj, line 29 and sample line 29, Peter Cabaj.

180. Interviews (S.E.D.).
    1950 U.S. Census, Michigan, Wayne County, Detroit, E.D. 85–1547, sheet 4, family 42, household of John Quinn, line 24, Dorothy Quinn.

181. Interviews (S.E.D.).

182. Wayne County, Michigan, Marriage Certificate of Peter Paul Cabay and Dorothy Lucille Quinn, local file no. 791688.

183. Note spelling of his name on marriage certificate.

184. Interviews (S.E.D.); Rutland Street address given on son Peter's death certificate (cited below).

185. Interviews (S.E.D.).

186. Interviews (S.E.D.); *Labyrinth 1970* (Redford: Bishop Borgess High School, [1970]), p. 145 ("M. Cabay") and p. 166 ("Susan Cabay"); *Labyrinth 1971* (Redford: Bishop Borgess High School, [1971]), p. 140 ("Cabay M"); *Labyrinth '72* (Detroit: Bishop Borgess High School, [1972]), p. 154 ("Mary Cabay"); *Labyrinth '77* (Redford: Bishop Borgess High School, [1977]), p. [161] ("Cathy Cabay"); *Labyrinth 1978* (Redford: Bishop Borgess High School, [1978]), p. 143 ("Cathy Cabay"); *Labyrinth 1979* (Redford: Bishop

Borgess High School, [1979]), p. 211 ("Catherine T. Cabay").

187. Oakland County, Michigan, Recorder of Deeds, Liber 7300, p. 233, 27 July 1978, filed 31 August 1978.

188. Interviews (S.E.D.).

189. Interviews (S.E.D.).

190. Peter Paul Cabay memorial stone, St. Hedwig Cemetery, Dearborn Heights, Wayne County, Michigan; Oakland County, Michigan, Death Certificate of Dorothy Lucille Cabay, filed 15 September 2010.

   Dorothy was buried beside Pete; at the time of this writing, she did not have a memorial stone (Cemetery visit by Christopher D. Cook, 7 March 2025; St. Hedwig Cemetery staff, telephone conversation with Christopher D. Cook, 7 March 2025).

191. Wayne County, Michigan, Death Certificate of Peter Paul Cabay, filed 3 February 1999; "[Death Notice of Peter P. Cabay]," *Detroit Free Press*, 4 February 1999, p. 4B.

192. Wayne County, Michigan, Marriage Certificate of Peter Paul Cabay and Dorothy Lucille Quinn, local file no. 791688.

193. Oakland County, Michigan, Death Certificate of Dorothy Lucille Cabay, filed 15 September 2010; "[Death Notice of Dorothy Cabay]," *Detroit Free Press*, 9 September 2010, p. 18A.

194. Interviews (unless otherwise noted).

195. Wayne County, Michigan, Death Certificate of Peter Cabay, Jr., filed 21 September 1951.

196. "Parent, Theodore 'Ted' 'Gene'," *Detroit Free Press*, 17 September 2006, p. B6; Eugene T. Parent memorial stone, Great Lakes National Cemetery, Holly, Oakland County, Michigan.

197. Wayne County, Michigan, Death Certificate of Timothy Paul Cabay, [no date filed given].

198. "Catherine Black Obituary," Legacy.com, https://www.legacy.com/us/obituaries/detroitnews/name/catherine-black-obituary?id=42736780; Catherine T. Black memorial stone, Great Lakes National Cemetery, Holly, Oakland County, Michigan.

# Illustration Credits

Page 13: *SVG > poland polish*. SVG SILH. https://svgsilh.com/image/1859706. html. Cropped and color modified. Public domain.

Page 15: RootOfAllLight. *File:Celtic knot cross.svg*. 7 October 2022. Wikimedia Commons. https://commons.wikimedia.org/w/index.php?title=File:Celtic_knot_cross.svg&oldid=852282480. Color modified. Creative Commons Attribution-Share Alike 4.0 International license (https://creativecommons.org/licenses/by-sa/4.0).

Page 17: Fredericks, Marshall. *The Spirit of Detroit*. 1958. Bronze and marble. Coleman A. Young Municipal Center, Woodward Avenue, Detroit. Photograph by VoxLuna, 24 June 2017. Wikimedia Commons. https://commons.wikimedia.org/w/index.php?title=File:Detroit_Spirit_at_night.png&oldid=1029209403. Creative Commons Attribution-Share Alike 4.0 International license (https://creativecommons.org/licenses/by-sa/4.0).

Page 18: *Background map:* SANtosito. *File:Subcarpathian Voivodeship Relief location map.svg*. 24 April 2018. Wikimedia Commons. https://commons.wikimedia.org/w/index.php?title=File:Subcarpathian_Voivodeship_Relief_location_map.svg&oldid=1021194635. Cropped and modified to include locator pins, placenames, and scale. Creative Commons Attribution-Share Alike 4.0 International license (https://creativecommons.org/licenses/by-sa/4.0). *Inset map:* TUBS. *File:Podkarpackie in Poland (+rivers).svg*. 30 November 2011. Wikimedia Commons. https://commons.wikimedia.org/w/index.php?title=File:Podkarpackie_in_Poland_(%2Brivers).svg&oldid=442686736. Creative Commons Attribution-Share Alike 4.0 International license (https://creativecommons.org/licenses/by-sa/4.0).

Page 19: Kurella, Ludwik. *W małym miasteczku [In a Village]*. About 1880. Oil on canvas, 65.5 × 113 cm. Sold at auction by Desa Unicum, Warsaw, Poland, 14 December 2017, lot no. 25. Wikimedia Commons. https://commons.wikimedia.org/w/index.php?title=File:Ludwik_Kurella_-_W_małym_miasteczku.jpg&oldid=1026854286. Cropped. Public domain.

Page 25: Catholic Church, Łączki Kucharskie Parish (Ropczyce, Podkarpackie, Poland). *Księgi metrykalne parafii rzymskokatolickiej Łączki Kucharskie [Parish Register Books of the Roman Catholic Parish of Łączki Kucharskie]*. Małżeństwa [Marriages], p. 649, no. 3, marriage record of Andrzej Cabaj and Marianna Skóra, 18 June 1888. Digital image at: Skanoteka – Metryki: Baza skanów akt metrykalnych [Database of Scans of Vital Records], Collection: 11094, Unit: 1888 / UMZ-1888, Unit Description: Marriages, File: 002, https://metryki.genealodzy.pl/id3312-sy1888-kt2. Cropped. Public domain.

Page 26: Catholic Church, Łączki Kucharskie Parish (Ropczyce, Podkarpackie, Poland). *Księgi metrykalne parafii rzymskokatolickiej Łączki Kucharskie* [*Parish Register Books of the Roman Catholic Parish of Łączki Kucharskie*]. Urodzenia [Births], p. 841, no. 31, birth record of Władysław Cabaj, 18 July 1889. Digital image at: Skanoteka – Metryki: Baza skanów akt metrykalnych [Database of Scans of Vital Records], Collection: 11094, Unit: 1889 / UMZ-1889, Unit Description: Births, Years: 1889, File: 012, https://metryki.genealodzy.pl/id3312-sy1889-kt1. Cropped. Public domain.

Page 28: *Poland, Church Books, 1568–1990*. "Petrus Szymaszek, Marriage." https://www.familysearch.org/ark:/61903/1:1:6VQ9-YX7X. Cropped. Public domain.

Page 31: Sąd Powiatowy w Dębicy [Dębica District Court]. Akta sprawy spadkowej po Franciszce Szymaszek z Paszczyny, zmarłej 1 sierpnia 1928 [Inheritance Case Files of Franciszka Szymaszek of Paszczyna Who Died on 1 August 1928]. Archiwum Państwowe w Przemyślu [State Archives, Przemyśl, Poland], A293/28. Digital copy in the collection of Christopher D. Cook. Used by permission of State Archives, Przemyśl, Poland (email message to Christopher D. Cook, 5 May 2025).

Page 32: Collection of Christopher D. Cook. Public domain.

Page 33: *Detroit City Directory for the Year Commencing September 1st, 1912*. Detroit: R. L. Polk & Co., 1912. Cropped. Public domain.

Page 35: Collection of Susan Eileen (Cabay) Delmotte. Public domain.

Page 36: U.S. District Court, Eastern District of Michigan, Southern Division. *Michigan, Wayne County, Naturalization Records, 1837–1999*. Naturalization petitions and records, v. 337, no. 83250–83500 (1934), records of Władysław Cabaj (FSL DGS 102198791, image 940 of 1125). Cropped. Public domain.

Page 39: Nicol, Erskine. *An Ejected Family*. 1853. Oil on canvas, 50 × 82 cm. National Gallery of Ireland, object no. 8749. Wikimedia Commons. https://commons.wikimedia.org/w/index.php?title=File:An_Ejected_Family_.PNG&oldid=1052998408. Cropped. Public domain.

Page 40: Nilfanion. *File:Island of Ireland relief location map.png*. 15 April 2012. Wikimedia Commons. https://commons.wikimedia.org/w/index.php?title=File:Island_of_Ireland_relief_location_map.png&oldid=1040624984. Modified to include locator pins, placenames, and scale. Creative Commons Attribution-Share Alike 3.0 Unported license (https://creativecommons.org/licenses/by-sa/3.0).

Page 42: *Ireland, Birth and Baptism, 1763–1917*. County: Mayo, parish: Ballina (Kilmoremoy), year range: 1879–1891, folio 55, no. 669, birth and baptism record of Joannes Joseph Quinn, 1 and 3 August 1882 (image 116 of 344), https://www.ancestry.com/imageviewer/collections/6068/images/41885_

b154747-00115. Cropped. Used by courtesy of The National Library of Ireland (NLI Reference No. RP 25/372).

Page 44: Collection of Christopher D. Cook. Public domain.

Pages 46–47, 50–53: Collection of Susan Eileen (Cabay) Delmotte.

Cover: *Photographs:* See credits for pages 35, 46, and 50. *Background map:* Reichspostamt. *Karte der grossen Postdampfschifflinien im Weltpostverkehr* [*Map of the Major Postal Steamship Lines in World Postal Traffic*]. Berlin: Reichspostamt, 1899. David Rumsey Map Collection, David Rumsey Map Center, Stanford Libraries, list no. 15829.001. https://www.davidrumsey.com/luna/servlet/s/sx0dgm. Cropped. Public domain. *Detroit map:* Rand McNally and Company. *Rand, McNally & Co.'s Indexed Atlas of the World: Map of Detroit and Vicinity.* Chicago: Rand McNally, 1897. David Rumsey Map Collection, David Rumsey Map Center, Stanford Libraries, list no. 3565.119. https://www.davidrumsey.com/luna/servlet/s/7ol5kh. Cropped. Public domain.

# Index

Cabaj, Pryska *see* Mądro, Pryska

Cabaj, Rozalia *see* Misiura, Rozalia

Cabaj, Walter 13, 19, 25–26, 32–38, 49, 54

Cabaj, Wawrzyniec 12, 21, 23–24

Cabaj, Władysław *see* Cabaj, Walter

Cabaj, Wojciech 24, 33

Cabaj, Zofia (b. 1785) *see* Litak, Zofia

Cabaj, Zofia (b. 1817) 21

Cabay (surname) 49

Cabay, Catherine Theresa 16, 51, 55

Cabay, Cecelia Helen 13, 34, 37, 38

Cabay, Clara Theresa 13, 38

Cabay, Dorothy Lucille *see* Quinn, Dorothy Lucille

Cabay, Mary Magdalene 13, 38

Cabay, Mary Margaret 16, 47, 51, 55

Cabay, Peter Paul 9, 12–13, 16–17, 19, 21, 27, 37, 38, 49–55

Cabay, Peter, Jr. 16, 49, 54

Cabay, Susan Eileen 16, 49, 51, 53, 54

Cabay, Timothy Paul 16, 51, 55

Cadillac Clark Street (Detroit) 49

Carpathian Mountains 21

Catholic Church 9, 10, 27, 51

Chicago, Illinois 19

Chrysler 51

Clare, Ireland 41

Cleveland, Ohio 19

Cloghan, Ireland 10, 43

Cobh, Ireland 40, 45

Cook, Aidan James 17, 54

Cook, Christopher Duane 16, 54

Cook, Lily Susannah 17, 54

Cork, Ireland 45

Corktown, Detroit, Michigan 46

County Clare, Ireland *see* Clare, Ireland

County Longford, Ireland *see* Longford, Ireland

County Mayo, Ireland *see* Mayo, Ireland

County Offaly, Ireland *see* Offaly, Ireland

County Roscommon, Ireland *see* Roscommon, Ireland

County Sligo, Ireland *see* Sligo, Ireland

Cudecka, Agnieszka 21

Czubczyński, Marianna 12, 28

Daley, Agnes Elizabeth *see* Quinn, Agnes Elizabeth

Daley, Catherine E. *see* Quinn, Catherine E.

Dearborn Heights, Michigan 37, 51

Dębica County, Poland 27

Dębica, Poland 27

Delmotte, Emily Catherine 16, 54

Delmotte, Jackson Patrick 17, 54

Delmotte, James Joseph 16, 54

Delmotte, Joseph Cabay 16, 54

Delmotte, Liv Sue 17, 54

Delmotte, Mason James 17, 54

Delmotte, Rachel Elizabeth 16, 54

Delmotte, Susan Eileen *see* Cabay, Susan Eileen

Delmotte, Vanessa Nicole *see* Mitchell, Vanessa Nicole

Detroit, Michigan 9, 10, 19, 33–34, 37–38, 45–47, 49, 54

Deyell, Margaret Cecelia *see* Quinn, Margaret Cecelia

Dolan, Bridget 14, 43

Dombkowski, Mary Magdalene *see* Cabay, Mary Magdalene

Draft, military 37, 46, 49

Dublin, Ireland 40

Dziedzic, Katarzyna 12, 22–23, 24

Dziedzic, Katarzyna (Mucha) *see* Mucha, Katarzyna

Dziedzic, Wawrzyniec 22

Ellis Island, New York 33, 34, 45

England 39

English language 10, 45

Famine, Irish 39
Ferbane, Ireland 41
Fisher Body Plant No. 10 (Detroit) 46
Ford Rouge Plant (Dearborn, Michigan) 37

Gaelic language *see* Irish (Gaelic) language
Galicia 19
Gallagher, Bridget 14, 41, 45
Gallen, Ireland 41
Gaweł, Józef 28
Gaweł, Teresa *see* Jedynak, Teresa
Gebbie, Frank 45
Gilligan (surname) 41
Gilligan, Anne *see* Guinan, Anne
Gilligan, Bridget *see* Kenny, Bridget
Gilligan, Bridget (b. about 1848) 42
Gilligan, Bridget (b. 1902) 43
Gilligan, Denis 43
Gilligan, James (b. about 1803 or 1804) 14, 42–43
Gilligan, James (b. 1896) 43
Gilligan, John 14, 42, 43, 47
Gilligan, Lucy 43
Gilligan, Margaret 43
Gilligan, Maria 42
Gilligan, Mary 15, 39, 43, 44–47, 49, 54
Gilligan, Mary (O'Brien) *see* O'Brien, Mary
Gilligan, Thomas 42
Glinik, Poland 10, 18, 21, 22, 23, 24, 27, 37
Great Britain 39
Great Depression 34
Grzegorski, Błażej 12, 28
Grzegorski, Katarzyna 12, 28–29
Grzegorski, Marianna *see* Czubczyński, Marianna
Guinan, Anne 14, 43, 47

Guinan, Bridget *see* Dolan, Bridget
Guinan, Hugh 14, 43
Guinan, Margaret 45

Hamburg America Line 32
Highland Park, Michigan 46
Holy Sepulchre Catholic Cemetery (Southfield, Michigan) 46
Hunter, Anne 14, 41–42, 47
Hunter, Bridget *see* Gallagher, Bridget
Hunter, James 14, 41
Hunter, Mary 45
Huron Township, Michigan 47

Independence Township, Michigan 16, 55
Ireland 9, 39–41, 45, 51
Irish (Gaelic) language 39, 41, 45
Irish Famine *see* Famine, Irish

Jamaica 51, 52
Jedynak, Maciej 27
Jedynak, Teresa 12, 27–28
Jedynak, Zofia 27

Kenny, Bridget 42
Kilmoremoy, Ireland 41, 42
Kilrehan Cemetery, Kincora, Ireland 43
Kincora, Ireland 43
King's County, Ireland *see* Offaly, Ireland
Kraków, Poland 21
Kramarz, Jadwiga 22
Kramarz, Marianna 24, 33
Kurcz, Veronica *see* Szymaszek, Veronica
Kurella, Ludwik 19
Kusibab, Maciej 29
Kusibab, Marianna *see* Paruch, Marianna

Łączki Kucharskie, Poland 10, 18, 21,

87

# Acknowledgments

This book would not have been possible without the resources available through FamilySearch (familysearch.org), Ancestry.com, Geneteka (geneteka.genealodzy.pl), IrishGenealogy.ie, and others.

I am indebted to numerous librarians and archivists who provided information on request including Marcin Walczak at Archiwum Państwowe w Przemyślu [State Archives, Przemyśl, Poland]; Madison Haack at the Bentley Historical Library, University of Michigan; staff at the Cadillac Wexford Public Library, Cadillac, Michigan; and staff at the National Archives and Records Administration.

Staff at St. Hedwig Cemetery, Dearborn Heights, Michigan, answered numerous questions. Dave Nowicki, via the PolishOrigins Forum (forum.polishorigins.com), offered guidance about translating Latin language entries in Polish records.

Lastly, but most importantly, descendants of Pete and Dorothy answered my questions, offered information and clarifications, and provided photographs. They also have welcomed me into the family and I am grateful that my children have such warm and loving relatives.

—C.D.C

www.ingramcontent.com/pod-product-compliance
Lightning Source LLC
Chambersburg PA
CBRC100736150426
42811CB00070B/1911

* 9 7 8 0 9 9 9 9 1 1 3 7 3 8 *